Radge Logic

Trading Thoughts and Wisdom

NICK RADGE

RADGE
PUBLISHING

First published in Australia in 2022 by Radge Publishing

ISBN: 978-0-9808128-6-2

© Nick Radge 2022
nick@nickradge.com

Radge Publishing
PO Box 721 Noosa Heads QLD 4567 Australia
www.radgepublishing.com

WELL AS FOR YOU. THE USE OF LEVERAGE CAN LEAD TO LARGE LOSSES AS WELL AS GAINS.

This brief statement cannot disclose all the risks and other significant aspects of securities and derivatives markets.

IT IS YOUR RESPONSIBILITY TO CONSULT YOUR FINANCIAL ADVISOR TO DETERMINE WHETHER TRADING IN SECURITIES AND DERIVATIVES PRODUCTS IS APPROPRIATE FOR YOU IN LIGHT OF YOUR FINANCIAL CIRCUMSTANCES

Table of Contents

Preface

For some 20-years I have attempted to write a weekly article about trading, trading systems, the market, technical analysis and other aspects of the business I have been involved in since 1985.

Some of these articles received significant feedback and comment. Others, not so much. The list of followers receiving these articles has steadily risen over the years – I only wish trends were as smooth as the growth seen in reader interest.

This book is a compilation of some of those articles. These are not necessarily the best, or worst, but they are designed to offer insights into my thinking about the markets and all things trading. While a full list of articles can be found on our website, we felt a published version of some of those may be useful for those that like to read a hard-copy or scribble notes and thoughts in the margin.

Trading has been a wonderful career for me but I can truly say that success has come from the strong support of Trish, not only as a wife, business partner and best friend, but also her organisational skills and business acumen. This book is dedicated to her and the wonderful joy she has brought me, our family and our friends, for many years.

Love you babe.

Nick

PRACTICAL TRADING GUIDE

Understanding Commission Drag

The number 1 reason why people fail at trading?

It has nothing to do with a trader's strategy. It has nothing to do with the fact they are trend following, short term trading, swing trading or scalping.

The number 1 reason people fail at trading is because they're undercapitalised.

All trading suffers drag via commission, so you must work backwards.

Let's assume that your trend following strategy makes fifty transactions a year. So that's fifty buys, fifty sells or a total of one hundred transactions a year. Now let's assume you pay ten dollars per transaction. That's a thousand dollars in commission for the year.

If you have a $10,000 account, you need to make 10% just to break even.

And 10% is too much drag.

If your account is smaller, let's say it's $5000, then you need to make 20% return just to breakeven.

This is not about strategy. It's about mathematics; the drag.

I don't care how good your strategy is, if you've got to make 20% to breakeven, you're pushing it uphill.

I've come across people who are actively trading, who need to make 40% just to breakeven.

If your commission drag is more than 5%, you've got to make a choice. You've either got to increase your capital, or decrease the commission rate you're paying, or a combination both.

Or stop trading until you have enough capital.

There is no point proceeding in this game if you've got to make 20% just to breakeven. It's an impossible, unrealistic goal.

If commission drag is more than 5%, you've got to act. Stop trading until you can get your commission drag down. Trading is hard enough as it is. You've got to make it as easy as possible, and there are things you can do.

It surprises me how many people cannot be bothered to change brokers, even though a change of broker can cut your commission cost by up to 70%.

Some brokers now offer 'commission free' trading. Let me assure you, nobody does anything for free, especially in this business. If you're thinking of using a commission free broker, ensure you read the fine print and assess the real costs.

The effort to change brokers may mean the difference between success and failure.

If you don't have enough capital; save more capital. I don't suggest borrowing money. If you don't have enough capital, you shouldn't be trading. The market's always going to be there so it's a matter of being patient and waiting until you're in a better position to make it mathematically possible to make money.

How Much Capital Do I Need to Start Trading?

We hear that some 95% of traders fail. Various central banks and financial regulators have done audits on broker accounts and have come to the same conclusion.

Why do traders fail?

There are probably several reasons including lack of strategy, lack of discipline and patience.

But in my view the biggest mistake is wanting to be a certain type of trader without understanding what is required to mathematically gain an edge.

Specifically, a lack of trading capital and the impact of commissions are the problem.

Many people come to trading with illusions of grandeur, excitement, and the thrill of the game so they naturally gravitate to shorter-term trading. Short term trading also adds to the 'instant gratification' mentality that is prevalent in society today.

There is nothing inherently wrong with short term trading, but it does lend itself to high turnover, usually 200 or more trades per year. 200 trades per year chews up a lot of commission which in turn creates drag on your account. Added to this is the dilemma that most new traders start with limited capital and they're almost guaranteed to fail before they begin.

The following chart shows the required gain to simply breakeven. The x-axis is various account sizes, and the y-axis is the required return to breakeven. We are assuming a short-term trader does 200 trades per year at $10 commission and a longer-term trader does 30 trades a year at the same rate.

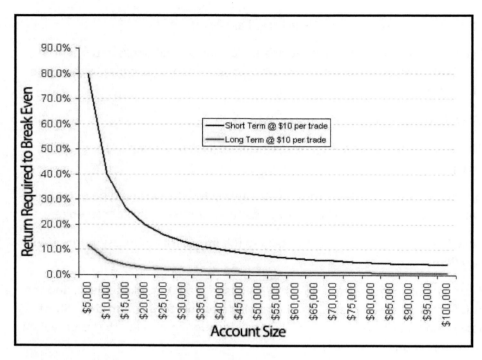

Not only is there a significant gap between the two, but the largest gap occurs between $5000 and $20,000, the account capitalisation of most new traders.

Even well-capitalised traders make the mistake of starting to trade using a lower amount of capital, "...I've got $X but I'll just start with $Y in case I fail". They create their own failure by doing so.

Rather than thinking "what type of trader do I want to be?" consider what capitalisation you must start with, what commissions your broker charges, and then decide what strategy would best fit. Use the chart above as a guide.

Create Your Own Trading Strategy

As much as we'd like to wake up one morning and be a better trader, taking your trading up a notch will take effort and work, like any other career.

From experience, I find the best way to move forward is to question everything then make it your own. Specifically, make minor adjustments to a core concept so it better suits your personality.

Regardless of how good a strategy might be, if it doesn't 'feel right' you won't be able to execute it.

Long term readers are aware of my 'aha!' moment in the early 90's after reading *PPS Trading System* by Curtis Arnold.

My trading progressed in the 18-months after reading that book because I made small adjustments to the strategy that not only made sense to me, but also made the execution of the strategy easier.

Comfort creates sustainability which in turn leads to long term success.

Sometimes making it your own means borrowing small bits and pieces from someone else. One of my weaknesses is not thinking outside the box. Thinking differently. Thinking up new ideas. Thankfully social media and blogs offer some great ideas.

Andrew Selby used to write a blog called *Don't Talk About Your Stocks*. In his quest for finding a robust trend following strategy, he stumbled across our Weekend Trend Trader strategy. But he had already been influenced by several authors such as Michael Covel and traders including the great William O'Neil. All their findings resonated with him, so he mixed the various pieces that made sense to him and came up with the Quantitative Growth Fund strategy.

But it didn't stop there.

In a conversation with Cesar Alvarez, a professional market researcher who had previously worked for Connors Research for many years, Andrew was introduced to historical volatility. Cesar was so intrigued with the simplicity and robustness of Weekend Trend Trader that he decided to run some tests with the inclusion of historical volatility. The results were even more promising, so much so that Andrew included the filter in his existing Quantitative Growth Fund model.

And so, it comes back to me. I hadn't heard of Cesar until my name started appearing alongside this research. I really hadn't explored historical volatility coupled with a trend following strategy such as our Growth Portfolio. I had researched it on shorter term time horizons, but nothing beyond a week's length.

That soon changed.

Question, test, validate, add, subtract, and tweak. Do whatever it takes to make a strategy your own.

Trading During Holidays

How should you manage your trades whilst on holidays?

Unfortunately, there is no simple answer.

For example, are you away for 2-days, 2-weeks or 2-months? Will there be reliable and secure internet access at your destination? Do you have a hand-held device that allows access? What are current market conditions?

TIP: Do not login to a trading account using free Wi-Fi. Preferably subscribe to a VPN service before you leave home.

Whilst each holiday will be different, here are some ideas.

A Real Holiday

Strange as it may sound, there is more to life than work and there is more to life than trading and the markets. If you're going away to unwind and recharge your batteries, then do exactly that - close all positions and turn your trading brain off. If you're touring several countries, the last thing you want to worry about is logging into your trading account at the next village.

The markets will be there when you return.

If you intend to sit under a palm tree sipping cocktails, make sure you only read fiction. Leave the trading books at home. Use your holiday to switch off and truly escape. You may not get the chance to relax for quite some time – so take advantage of it.

A Working Holiday

As trading is a business if you decide to trade whilst on holidays you are effectively on a working holiday. Things to consider will include:

- Is the market strong and trending well, for example, like we saw in late 2020 - 2021?
- Is it choppy and sideways, like it was in 2018 - 2019?
- What type of strategy are you trading; short term like the Power Setups® or longer-term positions like the Growth Portfolio?

> ☐ If you have short term positions and the market is strong you can place a stop loss, preferably at breakeven or better, and then roll that dice. I say 'roll the dice' because some of these positions may get stopped out whilst others may keep tracking well.

Remember: if there is corporate action during your holiday then all standing orders will be purged from the system - including your stop loss. This may be a problem.

Also, when trading US shares, take note of earnings releases. We recommend exiting any short-term positions ahead of any earnings releases, but if you're away then you may not realise the season is here. Remember that the US earnings season extends for a month or so and occurs each quarter. Unless you're trading the High Frequency Strategy, we recommend positions be closed before earnings.

Managing Longer-term strategies

Longer-term trends take time to develop and run their course. In certain circumstances failure to get on-board the rising trend near its start can be very costly. In other words, you need to do everything you can to catch the trend.

A personal example was 2020. I was lucky enough to go to cash on March 1st, just before the COVID crash. As at June 1st my account was about +3% for the year, but then my system signaled to go 100% long. I finished the year +50% for some portfolios and +97% for one portfolio. Had I been away when those trends began, I would have missed the significant gains and probably finished off with a mediocre year.

So, the issue when trading longer term is not so much managing open trades but missing out when big trends start.

In summary, I do not have an appropriate answer for the signal entries apart from standing aside. Relying on a friend or family member opens security issues as well as copyright/confidentiality breaches (if using The Chartist).

Managing a Longer-Term Portfolio

In terms of managing open positions within a longer-term portfolio, again we can exit if we feel dubious about the market trend however, I never like to close the door on positions simply for the sake of doing so. I'd rather allow the market to take me out of a position on the reversing trend.

If you use an 'on close' exit mechanism like we use for the Growth Portfolio, then maybe place a 'catastrophe stop' a fair distance away from current price action - something like 30% to 40%. This is a 'just-in-case' scenario which ideally won't come into play but would give you peace of mind that you'll be stopped out if something drastic occurs.

Managing longer-term trades really depends on your time away and connectivity. If you're only away for a week or even two, then I'd let the positions run their course. If trends are stronger then it is less likely any action will be required.

In early 2020 I travelled to Japan for a month and rarely logged into my account. The market was strong, and trends remained firm. I was content that not much untoward was going to occur. Longer-term systems allow more room so the impact of short-term gyrations in the trend tend not to generate signals.

If you have secure connectivity, even intermittently such as once a week, then I'd certainly let positions run and check in when you can. Being longer term in nature, it generally won't matter a great deal in the bigger picture if an exit is missed by a few days. The same is true for new entries. When we're looking for swings amounting to many dollars, a few cents here and there won't drag on performance.

Leverage and Position Sizing

The well-known 2% Rule, technically known as Fixed Fractional Position Sizing, enables us to correctly equalise risk across all positions. Any decent book or course that discusses risk management will highlight this form of risk management. However, in real time trading, specifically when it comes to trading equities, one learns very quickly that the amount of capital needed to fund positions using this technique will exceed the cash value of the account.

So, what to do?

There are a few suggestions.

Back in the days before leverage I came up with a filter known as the Bang-for-Buck filter. The Bang-for-Buck simply filters the relative volatility of the stock in comparison to its price.

To calculate the Bang-for-Buck filter, divide a $10,000 account by the closing price of the stock on any given day. This number is then multiplied by the average range of the stock for the last 200 days. The average range is the distance the stock has moved from high to low each day, including gaps, over the last 200-days. Dividing this number by 100 will convert the result to dollars and cents which in turn indicates the possible dollar return on any given day.

The higher the ratio, the higher the profit potential.

When faced with more opportunities than cash available, select stocks with higher Bang for Buck ratios.

This method works well if you only need to choose between a limited number of possible trades, but if you have a larger selection of trades, you really need to do the opposite. In our short-term Power Setups® Discretionary Portfolios we use a % Risk Filter which measures the risk on the trade to the underlying share price itself. Therefore,

%Risk Filter = (EntryPrice – StopLoss)/EntryPrice

Let's look at a selection of six random trades. Assume our account is $50,000 and we're willing to risk 1% on each trade.

Ideally if we're to follow the strategy as designed, we should be taking all six trades without question. However, as you can see, to take all six using Fixed Fractional of 1% will require capital of $104,123 – exceeding our available cash.

Ticker	Entry	Stop	% Risk Filter	Units to Trade	Value
MQG	60.90	59.55	2.22%	370	$22,556
JBH	17.47	18.21	4.24%	676	$11,804
ANZ	33.95	33.58	1.09%	1351	$45,878
FMG	4.65	4.30	7.53%	1429	$6,643
AZJ	4.85	4.65	4.12%	2500	$12,125
MML	1.74	1.57	9.77%	2941	$5,118
				Total Value:	$104,123

This table shows the relationship between the capital required and the % Risk Filter reading, specifically, the lower the reading the more capital is required to take a trade. ANZ has a reading of 1.09% reflecting the tight stop loss and the high underlying value of the share price. If we only had to select a single position, like we used the Bang for Buck Filter for, then we'd go with ANZ because we'd make a lot more profit for the same risk should the position move favourably.

However, in this case it's not about selecting a single trade. To gain diversification we need to take as many as we can with our limited capital.

To that end, we start with the highest %Risk Filter reading and work down to the lowest. Out of the six trades shown, we'd start with MML at 9.77%, then FMG, JBH, AZJ and finally we'll miss out on MQG, although we could take a half position. The four positions will use $35,690 worth of capital and allows us to take 4 of the 6 trades. This gives us some diversification and allows us to trade the strategy close to what was intended.

This process is fine if we have only 6 entries, but what if the market is ramping up with more opportunities and you want to put your foot down?

The answer is leverage.

** Warning – leverage can lead to large losses and gains and is not appropriate for everyone. **

The significant error many amateurs make with leverage is they use a top-down approach rather than a bottom-up approach.

A top-down approach goes something like this; we have $50,000 capital, and leverage to 75%. This means our own capital represents just 25% of the available funds we can access, and therefore we can now trade using $200,000. We can risk 1%, or $2000 on each trade.

The issue is that the $2,000 represents 4% of our actual capital which is well and truly above a reasonable and safe level.

If we use the table of trades above and assume all 6 get stopped out at their respective stop levels, our account would be at -24% before we even blink. Maybe not financially, but psychologically it's game over.

What we want to do is use a bottom-up approach instead, meaning we size our positions from our own $50,000 of capital, but use the leverage to facilitate all the trades. Our 6 trades require a total of $104,123 which is well within the level of leverage provided so we can take all 6. Should all 6 positions get stopped out we lose $3,000, or just 6% of our capital, which is in stark contrast to losing 24% on the same trades.

So, in summary, we have a variety of ways to determine which trades to take based on capital levels. However, the most efficient way to trade, allowing the most diversification with lower risk, is using leverage to facilitate the trades.

REMINDER: ** leverage can lead to large losses and gains and is not appropriate for everyone. **

"Risk Management is a Cop out…"

That's a quote from a value investor aimed at technical traders, specifically trend followers. His logic goes something like this:

If you can't pick good stocks then you're basically an incompetent investor, or, if you can pick good stocks then you don't need risk management.

True? False? Or, who cares so long as you turn a profit?

I'm in the latter camp but (because the Boss says I can't go fishing today) we'll talk it through. First, let's define what risk really is. When it comes to investing, risk has many faces, such as:

> → Market risk
> → Sector risk
> → Portfolio risk
> → Toxic position risk
> → Strategy risk
> → Liquidity risk, etc.

But at the end of the day, these all point to one thing – capital risk, or the risk of losing an uncomfortable amount of your capital. After all, most stories coming out of the GFC or the COVID crash were not about the risks listed above, but more so that people simply lost a boat load of money, and most people that throw in an investment tend to be influenced by the losses incurred. So loss of capital IS a key driver in investment decisions.

Capital risk is drawdown – the decline in your equity from a peak to a trough, and the largest decline in an investment is known as the Maximum Drawdown (MaxDD). The following table shows the annual rate of return (AROR) of some top Australian fund managers during the Global Financial Crisis and the capital losses their funds incurred.

	AROR	MaxDD
All Ordinaries Accumulation Index	8.78%	-51.40%
Argo Investments	8.20%	-44.69%
Hunter Hall Value Growth	14.70%	-45.94%
Prime Value Growth	14.90%	-35.70%
Colonial First State Aust. Shares	12.08%	-43.75%
FirstChoice High Growth	2.54%	-48.38%
Investors Mutual Aust. Shares	6.52%	-40.00%
ING Aust. Shares	7.06%	-45.65%
PM Capital Aust. Shares	6.88%	-50.00%
Schroder Aust. Equity	7.83%	-44.18%
Perennial Value Aust. Shares	7.89%	-42.85%
Berkshire Hathaway	8.95%	-56.36%
Legg Mason Value Growth	6.32%	-76.07%

When looking at risk and return together, the equation should be, "Are you willing to risk X% of capital to make Y% annual return?"

In the case of Argo Investments, the equation above is, "Are you willing to risk 44.69% of your capital to make 8.2% annual return?"

Without doubt an interesting and somewhat uncomfortable question. It does suggest however that not much thought has gone into risk management as most managers are not much better than a buy and hold investor.

But there is more to it, as we'll get too shortly. First however, let's look at toxic position risk. Toxic position risk occurs when you fall in love with a position, a company or a story about a company. A little like love, the investor gets blinded and is unable to make a rational decision. Here's a snippet of history showing a great example with the demise of HIH Insurance. The commentary is from the insurance analyst at JB Were back in 2000 who just couldn't give up on it:

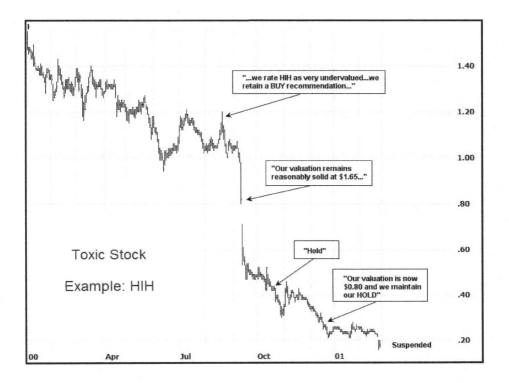

I think everyone has had one of these in their portfolio at some stage, but riding a loser into the ground, whether it be HIH, OneTel, Babcock & Brown, or even a Billabong, can do extensive damage to your portfolio.

Not being an expert stock picker, I need to rely on a mathematical edge to generate profits. The easiest way, albeit not necessarily the most comfortable, is to be a trend follower. The simple philosophy is to cut losses and let profits run. Agreed – it's not very edgy. Not very cool. And certainly, doesn't make a person look overly intelligent.

But it works.

So rather than focus on picking the next best thing, trend following works by maximising your wins when you win and minimising your losses when you lose. You'll come out ahead in the long run and you certainly won't have a situation like HIH. Get out of bad positions quickly, take a small loss, then

15

move on. Once you get a runner, then it's a matter of staying with it and not being tempted to take a small profit to recover a set of prior small losses. Remember, you'll never make a large profit by taking small profits.

Risk management is also about increasing the effectiveness of your trading once you do have an edge. It's about having optimal exposure to the market and to individual positions. Having a sub-optimal exposure will lead to dramatically reduced profitability, more so if you have a good edge.

Don't Believe the Rumours: Size Does Matter

When it comes to risk management there are two rules:

The Timid Trader Rule – "If you don't risk very much, you don't make very much."

and

The Bold Trader Rule – "If you risk too much, you go broke."

There are a few other guidelines which we'll discuss below, but the question for now is, "How much risk do I use?"

In the previous chapter 'Risk Management Is A Cop Out' I put forward that risk management is all about limiting the loss of your capital. That's the core goal, but to ensure we don't become a Timid Trader or a Bold Trader, we need to also ask the question, "How many shares/contracts should I buy/sell in order to get an optimal return for my desired risk tolerance?"

The 'how many' question is known as position sizing. But the answer is not so simple, mainly because it depends on the style of trading you're doing. There are many ways to determine how many shares to buy, but we'll focus on the two basic methods: fixed dollar and fixed fractional.

Fixed Dollar is straight forward and very easy to use. Simply divide your capital into equal parts, such as 10 or 20, and then buy that portion of shares.

If you have a $100,000 account, you will divide it into 20 equal parts of 5% and buy $5,000 worth of shares as each signal comes along. Simple, but not necessarily the most efficient way due to the volatility of different shares. Buying $5,000 of ANZ Bank for $32.00 that on occasion may move 1% in a day, is not the same as buying $5,000 worth of XYZ Ltd for $0.20 that may move 10% on any given day. Volatility is not equalised meaning that one could make or lose a lot more than the other.

When using the Fixed Dollar approach, one needs to 'pigeonhole' risk by buying companies of the same breed, i.e., buying only blue chips, or buying only small caps, or buying only micro caps. In other words, don't mix blue chips with micro caps because you're simply exposing yourself to more risk and more volatility.

Fixed Fractional position sizing on the other hand does equalise risk, albeit it's somewhat more complicated to grasp and probably best for discretionary traders. This method is used when the distance between the entry and stop loss varies. For example, you may want to buy ANZ Bank at $33.00 with a stop loss at $32.00 or XYZ Ltd for $0.20 with a stop loss at $0.18. If the stop is triggered on ANZ you are exposed to a 3% decline in equity, but if the stop is hit in XYZ you're exposed to a 10% decline in equity. Therefore, you want to buy a lot more shares in ANZ to gain the same exposure as you would have in XYZ.

But, as per the Bold Trader Rule, losing 10% of your equity on a single trade will end your trading career very quickly.

We need to accept that a series of losses is possible (indeed extremely probable), so risking 10% of equity on a single trade opens the door to losing a large amount of our capital very quickly. Even a strategy that has a 90% success rate, will still be exposed to 5 losses in a row, or a 50% decline in capital. So obviously we need to scale that risk back to allow us to travel through a bad series of trades when they come.

The following table shows what a probable losing streak will look like dependent on the success rate of your strategy:

Win %	Probable Streak
30%	30
35%	25
40%	21
45%	18
50%	16
60%	12
70%	9
80%	7
90%	5

If we offer the market some humility and suggest we'd only be right 50% of the time, which many successful traders are, then we should expect to have 16 losing trades in a row at some stage. It may not happen for a week, a month, a year, or a decade, but mathematically it will happen. So, with that in mind we now need to ask ourselves how much of our capital are we willing to lose should the nasty losing streak hit?

So here's one of those guidelines I was going to mention...

The amount of capital decline you think you can handle is probably twice the amount you really can cope with in real life.

Losing money on paper is one thing. Losing money in reality is a very different ball game.

Let's assume you can handle an equity decline of 20%, and let's assume your strategy has a success rate of 60%. Therefore, you can expect to have a losing streak of 12 trades at some stage. As such you cannot risk any more than 1.6% of your account equity on any given trade (20/12 = 1.666).

Many textbooks will have you believe you can risk 2% on each trade, but at 2% you will have a drawdown of 24% – which is above your threshold.

Remember, when it comes to trading, the long-term winners are the best losers. In other words, winners don't blow their account up, or they don't get psyched out of trading due to a drawdown beyond their coping ability.

So assume we can risk 1.6% of our account on our hypothetical ANZ and XYZ trades. What we need to do to equalise risk at 1.6% is work backward to define how many shares to buy – the original question of risk management.

We'll buy ANZ at $33.00 with a stop loss at $32.00. Therefore,

> 1.6% of our $100,000 account is $1,600
> $1,600 / ($33.00 – $32.00) = 1600 shares with a value of $52,800

And for XYZ, buying at $0.20 with a stop loss at $0.18. Therefore,

> 1.6% of our $100,000 account is $1,600
> $1,600 / ($0.20 – $0.18) = 80,000 shares with a value of $16,000

Immediately you can see that to equalise risk we need to buy vastly different numbers and values of shares. Remember, we're equalising risk – not equalising the value of capital allocated to the trades. This example clearly shows the major shortfall when trading equities with this technique, i.e., we need to allocate half the account to facilitate the ANZ trade. So, if ANZ gets stopped out at $32.00 we lose 1.6% of our account balance. If XYZ gets stopped out at $0.18 we will also lose 1.6% of our account balance. Risk has now been equalised.

How many trades in a row can we have before we can't trade anymore? More than 150...

The reason is that because we're always risking 1.6% of our capital. This will ensure we're risking less dollars as our account declines. 1.6% of $100,000 is not the same dollar amount as 1.6% of $90,000. So as losses mount up it becomes harder to lose money. It's a natural defence mechanism.

And when we're winning, we naturally compound the account. 1.6% risk on $100,000 is not the same a 1.6% risk on $110,000.

When doing something right – do more of it. When doing something wrong – do less of it.

When we look at some hard data, we can see a well-defined difference. Below are the statistics and equity curves using the exact same trades – the difference is in the position sizing used. Risk Model A allocates a fixed $5,000 to each trade, whilst Risk Model B allocates a fixed fractional 1% risk to each trade. The latter grows at a much healthier rate, 3x the rate in fact, albeit it shows a little more volatility. Risk Model A, the fixed dollar allocation, is what many novices do.

Sure, it works. But it's not optimal.

Note also the commission drag – Model A needs to make a lot more just to cover commission costs than that of Model B. (See chart and table on following page.)

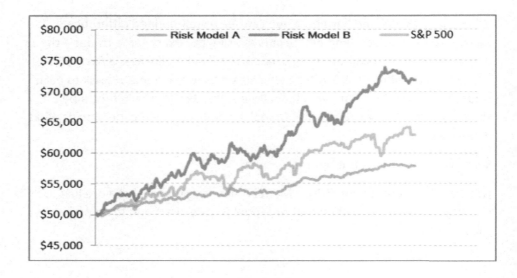

	Risk Model A	Risk Model B	S&P 500
Net P&L	$7,939	$21,868	$12,966
ROI	15.88%	43.74%	25.93%
MaxDD	-$906	-$3,333	
MaxDD (%)	-1.67%	-5.18%	-5.75%
# trades	321	321	
Win %	60.1%	61.1%	
Avg Win	$97	$301	
Avg Loss	-$84	-$298	
W/L Ratio	1.15	1.01	
Pfactor	1.74	1.59	
Comm's paid	$790	$790	
% of P&L	9.9%	3.6%	

20/20 Hindsight Trading System

I was mentoring a trader, let's call them MJ. They're inquisitive and don't mind being prompted to search for the answers rather than having them served up on a plate. An individual coming to the right conclusions themselves will have the lessons cemented firmly in their minds. After discussing how to find robust trading patterns, MJ dropped me an email with a pattern they'd found and ironically called 20/20.

Here's a chart of the equity growth:

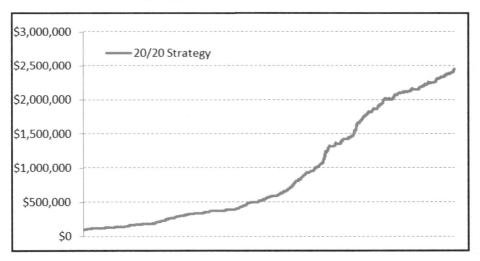

Looks impressive for sure. The winning percentage of trades is 63% and a win/loss ratio of 1.38. This equates to a 19.5% non-compounded return with a maximum drawdown of -7.5%.

But you know how it goes, "If it's too good to be true it usually is…"

The first giveaway is the smoothness of the equity curve, especially since this is a single market system, i.e., it only trades one market. This immediately suggests to me 'curve fit', but the rules suggest otherwise.

Entry:

Take the average of the last 20 session's highs. If the close is greater than that average, buy the next day at market.

Exit:

Exit at the close.

Simple. Robust. The sample has 2258 trades from 1995 through 2014 and is operated through all sorts of market conditions.

So, what's the issue?

The calculation done by the client contains a post-dictive error.

A post-dictive error simply means that we look at something that happens in the future to make a decision today. Obviously, we can't know what the future holds and therefore today's decision is prone to error. In this case MJ waited for today to close above the 20-day average high – exactly as the rules state, but instead of using tomorrow's open as the buying reference point, he used <u>today's</u> open – which has already occurred. He then used today's close at the exit reference point, and because today's high was above the 20-day average high it was always going to be a strong close.

A very simple mistake – but a very costly one. Let's look at the comparison between the two equity charts:

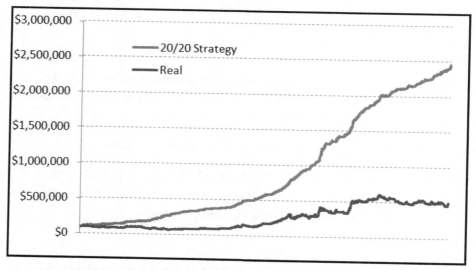

If we now drill into the correctly calculated system, we can gain some better insights into the reality of it:

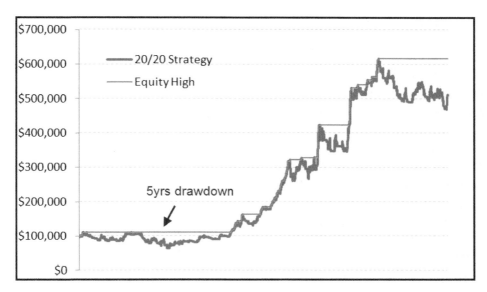

Now we see a very different and somewhat more distressing story. The strategy has 53% winning trades, with a win/loss ratio of 0.99. When playing with such a small win/loss ratio we either need to see the winning percentage of trades above 60% or a much higher frequency of trades, to gain some mathematical expectancy. The maximum equity decline is -42.3% with an annual return of 9.35%. Not very comfortable.

Post-dictive errors are quite common. We must remember the old computer programmer's motto: "Garbage in, garbage out." Rather than attempting to prove a strategy right, try and prove it wrong.

Nick Radge

A Powerful Entry Technique

I first started using this entry method back in the early 90's when I was testing the PPS Trading Strategy by Curtis Arnold. This entry is not part of that book, nor do I know its exact history. Testing the PPS patterns by hand for over 1800 hours showed me that this technique was a more definable way to enter the market and it offered a lower risk, higher reward proposition – if it was successful. However, it's not for everyone. It can, on occasion, be a frustrating technique and can lower the win rate. Many years after my initial research on PPS I noted Joe Ross was using a similar method, albeit in a different way, and as he'd named it already in his extensive body of work, I also applied the same name.

The technique is known as the **Traders Trick Entry (TTE).**

In the Bendigo Bank (BEN) chart below we can see a great example of a PPS micro triangle that has 4 distinct pivot points. Standard practice is entering on penetration of the lower boundary with a stop loss cutting through the centre of the pattern extending from the apex. In my view there are two issues with this setup. Firstly, as the entry point is in many trading texts we can assume that any trader looking at this pattern will also be looking to enter at the same point. If so, then the competing orders may increase slippage. The second issue is that the initial stop loss is not really based on any solid technical point of reference, i.e., it's not above any dedicated resistance or pivot high. It's just sitting inside the noise of the pattern.

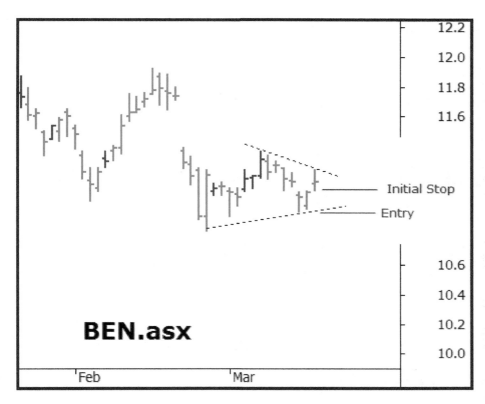

The TTE on the other hand attempts to remove both these concerns.

Consider the following chart.

 Rather than awaiting a downside penetration of the pattern we look to enter the trade as soon as prices start to swing lower. Once the 4th pivot is in place, we place an order to enter short 1c below this bar. This alleviates being caught up in any congestion at the pattern breakout, and if there are other orders sitting there, they'll actually help our cause. And the initial stop is placed 1c above the high of the 4th pivot, which will provide a better level of technical support should prices start to swing lower immediately.

We can never know if the pattern will complete. If prices move higher we can adjust the levels up until the pattern either invalidates or gets us into the trade. As mentioned above, the risk is an outside day; that is prices start lower triggering an entry, then reversing and taking out the initial stop. It happens. It is frustrating, but the ability to join a move with the lowest possible risk will always offer a greater reward.

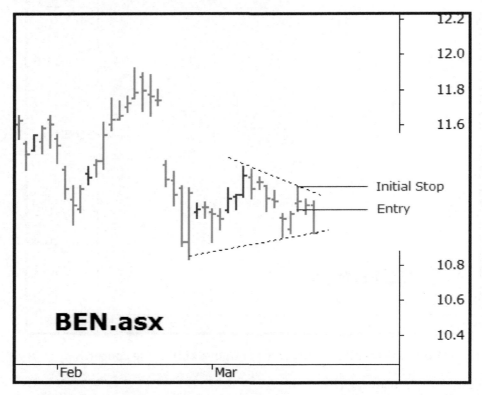

The following chart of Cinemark Holdings ($CNK) offers a picture-perfect bearish A-B-C pattern straight out of our Playbook. Whilst the pattern is complete, note that the colours of the bars are Green, indicating a bullish trend and therefore a short side trade is not yet warranted.

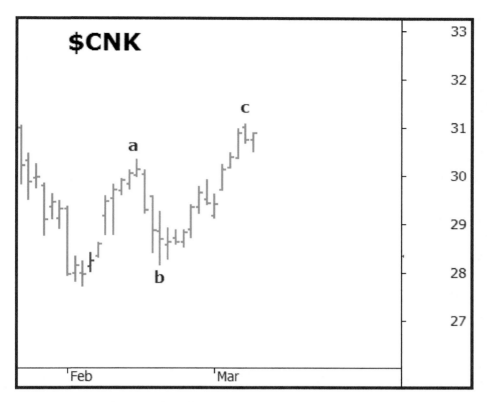

However, over the next few days the trend turns to neutral and then bearish which then allows a position to be taken should downside follow through occur. The TTE is usually a single bar pattern, specifically where the entry level is 1c below the low of the entry bar, and the stop loss is 1c above the high of the pattern. Because we have a slight transition in the trend, we don't get the single bar entry here, but it's still extremely tight between entry and stop loss enabling the lowest possible risk without using intraday or smaller time frames.

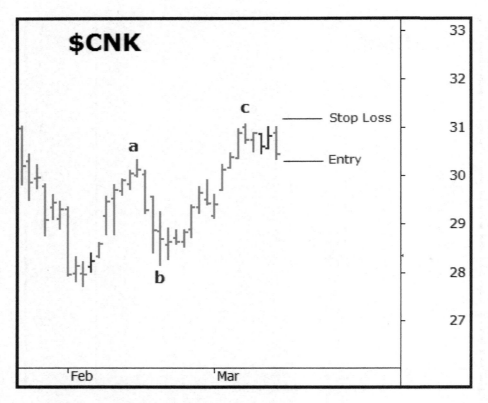

Next, we see that CNK drops in alignment with the broader market trend. The trade would now be managed accordingly.

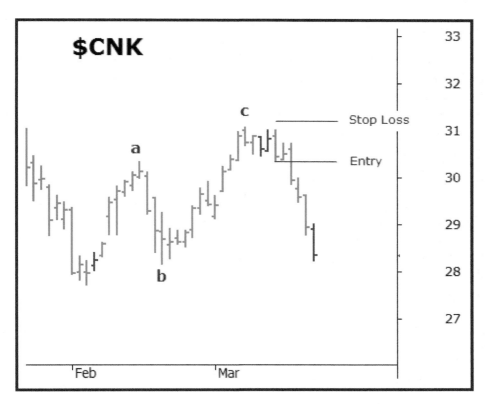

The TTE is extremely versatile and can be used on all 17 of our Playbook setups and can also be used when trading other types of patterns, including leaning on support and resistance.

Trading With Divergence

The world of technical analysis is saturated with indicators, oscillators, lines and other weird and wonderful esoteric attempts at finding the Holy Grail. However, there are just three absolutes: price, volume, and time. These items, coupled with patience and a level head for creating positive expectancy, enable us to be successful trading the market.

Divergence is a useful indicator, or method, to identify and trade trend reversal moves. Divergence occurs when price moves in one direction and the indicator starts moving in the opposite direction. There are three published versions of divergence known as Type-A, -B and −C. discussed by Dr Alexander Elder in his best seller, Trading for a Living. As the Type-A setup is the most powerful it's the only one that makes an appearance in our Playbook.

There are several indicators used to identify divergence including the MACD, RSI, Williams %R and Stochastic. The trick is to pick one indicator and stay with it and not be tempted to chop and change. Most indicators are used incorrectly and thus they tend to be futile when used in the real world. My indicator of choice for divergence is the Stochastic.

Let's define the Stochastic:

The Stochastic (Slow) indicator calculates the location of a current price in relation to its range over a period of bars. The default settings are the most recent 14 bars, the high and low of that period to establish a range and the close as the current price. This calculation is then indexed, smoothed, and plotted as SlowK. A smoothed average of SlowK, known as SlowD, is also plotted. SlowK and SlowD plot as oscillators with values from 0 to 100. The direction of the Stochastics should confirm price movement.

The following chart shows a Type-A Bearish Divergence on the daily chart of Medusa Mining (MML). Prices probe higher but the indicator fails to make a secondary higher high:

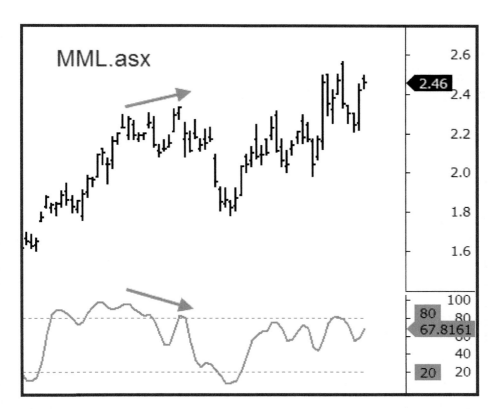

The key to trading divergence is it should be obvious to the naked eye. If you need to look closely at the chart to measure it, then it's probably best to stand aside and await a very clear example. When a divergence is in place we expect that prices have stretched too far to continue, and either must (a) consolidate for a period of time, or (b) snap back against the momentum. When we trade the setups, we're looking for the latter to profit.

Infomedia (IFM) offers a Type-A Bullish Setup whereby prices make a new low, but the Stochastic fails to confirm by making a higher low. Note how prices snapped back in the coming weeks.

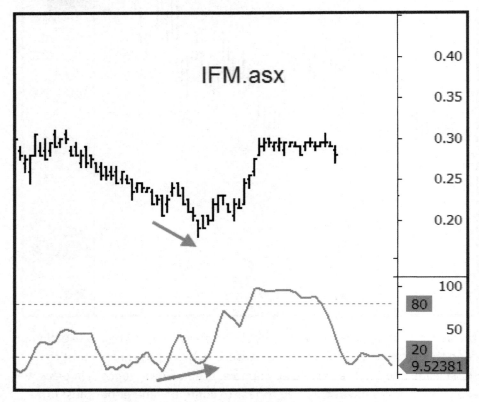

Being a reversal pattern, these divergences will be found predominantly against the trend of the broader market. If you're new to trading, or looking for a 'higher probability' outcome, then it's always best to trade aligned with that broader market trend rather than against it. This is very easily spotted and done using our short-term trend (see next chapter).

The previous example shows a Type-A Bullish setup for Intuit Inc ($INTU). Prices had been falling in alignment with the $SPX trend, but once that started turning higher $INTU had a quick spike to new lows to form the setup and then started a new bullish swing surpassing prior highs.

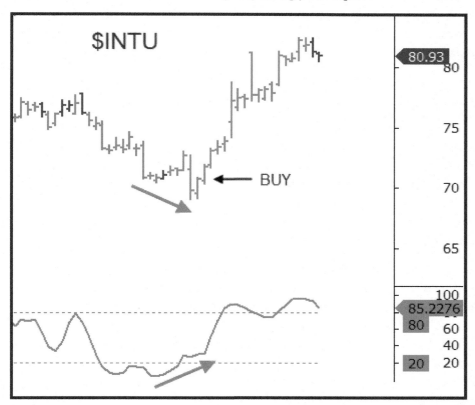

Nick Radge

Defining the Short-Term Trend

A great question came across my desk:

"...as a swing trader (1 – 10 days) I'm looking to buy shares when the market is going up in short bursts and then reverse and go short during the down moves. I would be interested in how to determine when to get in or out of the market..."

The Chartist ASX and US Power Setups® both contain a Discretionary Portfolio that does exactly that; specifically attempts to ride short term price movements both up and down.

The key with the short-term movements is to position oneself in the direction of the prevailing market trend, so if you're trading Australian stocks you may wish to align yourself with the trend of the All Ordinaries Index, or, if you're trading US stocks you should align yourself with the trend of the S&P 500. Don't get too caught up in the intricacies of which index to use, it's more important to align your position accordingly.

If you've read *Unholy Grails* you'll be familiar with the benefits of using a Regime or Index Filter. Simply put we defined the underlying trend of the broader market using a moving average. This concept is nothing new, indeed I was first introduced to it back in the early 90's after reading PPS Trading System by Curtis Arnold. He defined the trend of individual markets (as opposed to the broader market) by using two moving averages – the 40 day and the 18 day. He would then look for small consolidation patterns and trade on any respective breakout.

Over the years our research has suggested that using moving averages on smaller time frames, such as 1 – 10 days, is not an overly effective method – they tend to lag too much. The market gyrates quickly in this time frame so one can't afford to allow too much room for the market to move back and forth.

After researching extensively using computerised models and our own experience we found that using a Relative Strength Index (RSI) was significantly more attuned to the bends and twists of short-term volatility. Whilst the exact formula for our method is proprietary, we found the RSI on its own was too noisy, so we smoothed it then combined both the raw RSI and the new smoothed version together to define the trend.

The following chart shows the trend of the $SPX in three phases: green bars when the trend is up, red bars when the trend is down, and blue bars when there is a potential transition from one to the other.

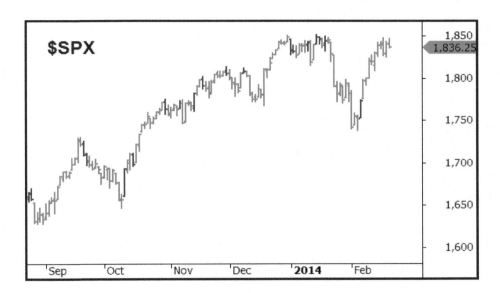

From here we then apply the trend filter to the individual stocks themselves. The next chart shows MSCI Inc ($MSCI) but it should be noted that the colour of the bars is related to the trend of the $SPX and not $MSCI itself. By doing so we can quickly see opportunities aligned with the broader market trend, but we can also see how the individual stock is performing relative to the broader market.

The next step is to combine the trend of the underlying market with one of the 17 setups that we like to trade from our Power Setups® Playbook.

The next chart shows a bullish Darvas Box setup in American Railcar ($ARII). During the construction of the pattern the trend of the $SPX went from bearish to bullish and therefore gave us the green light to take a trade on the long side.

The last chart in this article shows a short side trade that triggers from a break of a horizontal support setup from our Playbook. Ascent Capital Corp ($ASCMA) struggled to break into new high ground forming a double top, but then dived after the trend of the $SPX turned bearish as shown by the red bars. There was ample time to spot the setup and position accordingly.

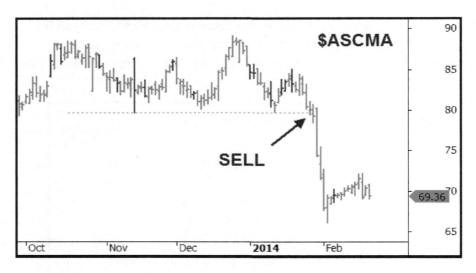

Trade Management with An Index Filter

In the previous chapter we discussed the importance of aligning oneself with the short-term trend when swing trading. Now we're going to look at how that same short term trend filter can improve trade management.

Before we jump in, it's imperative to mention the importance of exits and why they tend to be the determinant of profits, rather than the entries.

It's no secret that new and amateur traders strive for the perfect entry. There's a common fallacy that, to be successful in trading, we need to select the right stock, sector, market, or the right trade. The focus is on being right. As such trade selection or stock selection becomes the goal, as opposed to making money.

To highlight the inconsistency of attempting to select a better entry, here are two equity curves that both use the same entry setup, the same entry point, and the same position sizing. They've both made 300-odd trades, and both paid $2000 in commissions. The only difference is the exit used:

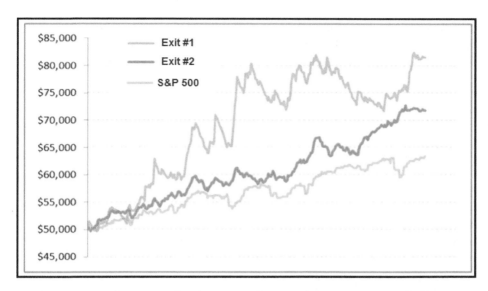

Several points of interest; firstly, Exit #1 has made 46% more profit than Exit #2 (63.1% vs. 43.5%). The win/loss ratio of Exit #1 is 2.5x that of Exit #2 (2.54 vs. 1.04). These are both very promising data points, and for the average trader wanting to make as much money as possible, they'd be inclined to use Exit #1. But the story changes somewhat when we dig beyond net profits and into the actual journey travelled to make those profits (a topic that long time readers of my material will be well versed in).

It's obvious that Exit #1 is more volatile than #2 – the equity jumps around like a roller coaster, whereas #2 shows a much smoother ascent. Secondly the win rate of Exit #1 is just 35%, in other words 2/3rds of all trades are losers.

Experience suggests that once the percentage of winning trades drops below 40% the task of following the system becomes psychologically more difficult. We can measure the 'difficulty of execution' using Profit Factor. Profit Factor is calculated by dividing the total net profits by the total net losses. The higher the Profit Factor, the easier the system is to trade. The Profit Factor for Exit #1 is 1.38 and considered quite low. Exit #2 on the other hand has a win rate of 61% and a Profit Factor of 1.61 making it more comfortable to trade.

Let's move to the Index Filter that we discussed last week and how it can be used to manage our trades. As an example we'll use a Resistance Line setup straight out of our Playbook:

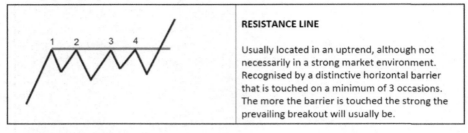

RESISTANCE LINE

Usually located in an uptrend, although not necessarily in a strong market environment. Recognised by a distinctive horizontal barrier that is touched on a minimum of 3 occasions. The more the barrier is touched the strong the prevailing breakout will usually be.

The following chart shows Unit Corp ($UNT) and a 3-point resistance line break. The initial break was not valid because our Trend Filter was still in the blue "Neutral" state. We would therefore enter on the next move higher when the Trend Filter was in the green "Bullish" state.

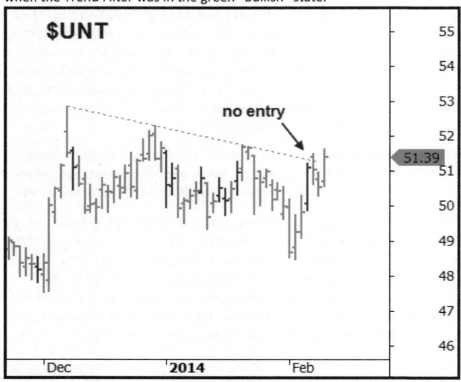

The next chart shows how $UNT pushed higher over the following weeks aligned with the trend of the S&P 500 (all green bars). Then, on March 3rd, the S&P 500 signalled a trend reversal from Bullish to Bearish, although it's not often we see a complete trend flip like this. Normally we'd see the blue Neutral come into play which allows a softer stop adjustment, such as a channel or count-back method.

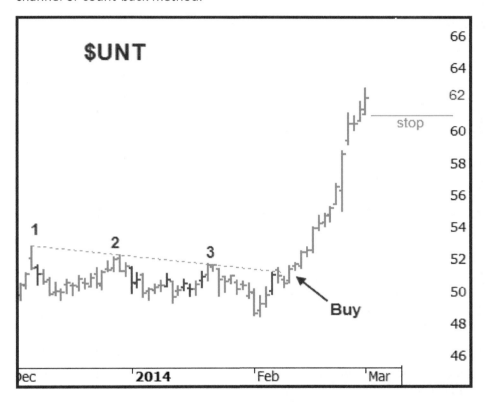

With the trend of the S&P now deemed Bearish we need to be more assertive with the trade management because probabilities suggest individual stocks will also retreat. I'm never one to completely close the door on a trade, meaning exiting just for the sake of exiting. I prefer that stocks 'take me out' by confirming price action. So, when the trend of the S&P 500 turns down and flashes a red bar, we will adjust the stop aggressively – right up and below the low of that day. If prices continue lower we'll be taken out of the trade and lock in the profit, but should prices buck the trend of the broader market we'll at least be able to stay on the ride without giving too much back.

Notice in the final chart that even though the Trend Filter flipped back to green, we did get taken out of the position on penetration of the low.

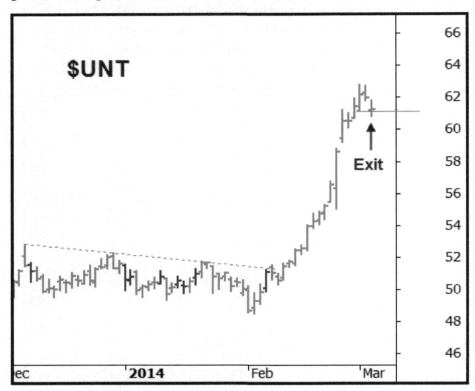

There could be some discretionary rules added to say that should the Trend Filter move back to the Bullish green state that we revert to a standard trailing stop, but that would involve moving the stop loss backward – which we never want to do.

Remember, our minds think and act differently when we have a position on, so it's imperative to stick with the rules throughout the process. We can always look back and assess past trade performance to make future adjustments, but not during a trade.

How to be Proactive with Position Sizing

Drawdowns, or a decline in equity from peak to trough, are part and parcel of trading.

How you cope with drawdowns will determine how successful you will be as a trader.

The famed Turtle Traders[1] used an interesting position sizing strategy, albeit I'm sure those surviving Turtles have modified this to some degree.

They were instructed to decrease the size of their trading account by 20% each time the strategy drawdown reached -10%.

So, if the starting capital was $100,000 and the account slips to $90,000, then, from that point on, position sizing would be based on an account size of $80,000.

If the account then slipped to $82,000 (0.10 * 90,000) then the account balance for position sizing would drop to $64,000.

Only after the account recovered to the prior levels would the account balance for position sizing revert back.

Personally, I don't use this technique, mainly because I use a fixed percentage allocation method and a systematic approach.

However, if you're a discretionary trader and use a fixed fractional position sizing model, then this could be a method to explore.

---

[1] https://www.turtletrader.com/

Nick Radge

Managing Larger Portfolios

For the last 20-years I have run my main trend following portfolio with 20 equal positions, each with 5% capital.

Most assume 20 is a nice round number, but in fact the efficient frontier for portfolio diversification is 18 positions. Rather than explain that to clients, and to make life easier, I simply rounded it to 20.

I recently received an interesting question from a client. Rob expressed concerns about getting fills as his portfolio had grown to a point that liquidity started to become an issue.

There are a few solutions to this, but let's start with Rob's initial query.

He asked what the returns looked like when the number of positions increased, to either 30 or 40.

To answer that we'll test the idea on the Weekend Trend Trader strategy, traded on the ASX using the default parameters. Commissions and dividends have been included as have delisted stocks via Norgate Data.

The chart below shows the equity growth using 10, 20, 30 and 40 positions.

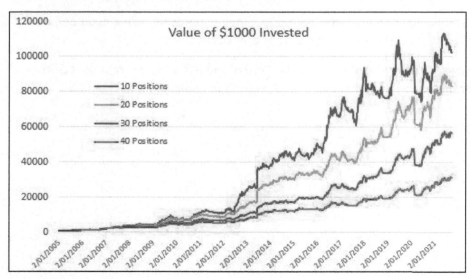

The higher the concentration of positions, the higher the return. However, that comes at a cost, portfolio volatility.

So, what's a good trade-off?

The table below shows a summary of various performance metrics. The MAR ratio measures the annual growth rate divided by the maximum drawdown (deepest equity decline). Essentially, it's measuring the risk-adjusted return, meaning the higher the number, the better the performance.

The 30-position portfolio offers a compounded growth rate of 27.27% with a maximum drawdown of -21.25%. That drawdown level circa -20%, tends to be a maximum level for most retail investors. So, Rob could increase his portfolio to 30 positions to help alleviate some of the liquidity issues without giving away too much of the return.

	10 Positions	20 Positions	30 Positions	40 Positions
Annual Return %	31.81%	30.23%	27.27%	22.86%
Exposure %	75.21%	73.76%	70.41%	67.20%
All trades	418	743	1087	1384
Transaction costs	7942	14117	20653	26296
Winners	208 (49.76 %)	390 (52.49 %)	562 (51.70 %)	684 (49.42 %)
Losers	210 (50.24 %)	353 (47.51 %)	525 (48.30 %)	700 (50.58 %)
Max. system % drawdown	-32.02%	-23.89%	-21.25%	-20.56%
MAR	0.99	1.27	1.28	1.11
Profit Factor	1.72	2.02	2.14	1.97
Win/Loss	1.74	1.83	2	2.02

However, there are two other ways to deploy capital when liquidity becomes an issue. The following are suggestions that I personally use.

The first is useful when trading longer-term trend or momentum strategies. Being longer-term in nature, slippage is not a large drag on performance. If we're holding positions for many months, and looking to capture big moves, then paying a few extra cents here and there isn't costly.

So, partial positions can be bought during the day without too much disturbance to liquidity. This is also more practical these days with flat fee or zero fee brokers.

The second is allocating funds across a variety of different strategies and markets. Obviously, this increases diversification, but also allows funds to be distributed more broadly.

Combining Trading Strategies to Diversify Your Portfolio

Julie B. asks:

"Have you run a test where you allocate equal amounts to [turnkey strategies]? If so, can you share the resulting data?"

I'm an avid proponent of diversifying across various systems. Indeed, I trade 8 systems currently that encompass various styles, time frames and geographical markets.

Julie's question is appropriate for those that may not have the time or capabilities of designing, building, and testing their own strategies.

For this example, we'll combine the following turnkey strategies (available from The Chartist's online shop):

- ▢ Large Cap Momentum
- ▢ Weekend Trend Trader
- ▢ Mean Reversion
- ▢ Day Trade (Long)

We'll use the default settings as per the performance test notes of each strategy. For ease of comparison, this test has only been conducted on US markets to alleviate any currency movements. No margin has been used.

The following equity chart shows the growth of each strategy and the combined strategy, where the capital was equally divided into 4 parts.

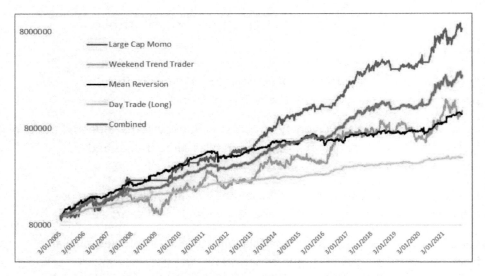

The combined equity growth (green) is certainly smoother, however there are some caveats.

Firstly, no re-balancing has been done. Ideally each portfolio should be re-balanced at least once a year. I would expect this will greatly enhance the risk/adjusted return and the smoothness of equity growth.

Secondly, the day trade strategy was designed to be used with leverage. Which is why it "appears" to underperform here. In the real world, assuming leverage is not used, one would weight the allocations according to the strategy volatility. As such, the Large Cap Momentum and Weekend Trend Trader would get lower allocations. The Mean Reversion and Day Trade strategies would get higher allocations.

DEFINING AND TESTING TRADING SYSTEMS

Buy the Open or Buy the Close?

All the strategies outlined in my trading books enter and exit positions at the open. This has prompted a reader question:

Hey Nick.

The accepted saying in many trading books and articles is that amateurs open the market, but the professionals close it.

I have seen many times a stock open high in the first hour of trading, but gradually retrace throughout the day until 4pm. Emotional inexperienced traders can often pay top dollar at or near the open.

Not sure if you have ever done any testing re buying at the close or open. With Growth Portfolio stocks some subscribers may prefer to buy at the close in order to see if the stock still has upward momentum. -Todd E.

A good question and an interesting observation. But like any observation we need to put it to the test to ensure we're not falling for recency or confirmation bias.

For this test we'll use a simple momentum strategy on the Russell-1000 universe. Momentum in this case was measured using a 200-day rate of change. No other filters are used.

The evidence suggests that buying on open has a slight edge over buying on close. I tested across various strategies in both the Australian and US markets and whilst the edge flipped between the two, it was only ever marginal one way or the other.

However, there are two other reasons why I tend to use the open. The first is that, in Australia, the market uses an opening auction. An algorithm is used to determine the volume on the buy side versus the volume on the sell side, as well as the prices at which they have been placed. This algorithm results in an official 'auction' price, which is the price at which the stock opens.

The benefit is twofold; it's one of the most liquid times of the trading session so slippage is limited, and secondly, it 100% ensures my real time results match the backtest result.

The other reason we employ the open auction is to simplify execution. Signals are generated after the close allowing some 18 hours to place orders for the next session. No screen watching and no special-order requirements needed.

The easier a strategy is to execute the more likely you'll continue to follow it.

The BBO Strategy 10-Years on

One of the most popular strategies in *Unholy Grails* was the Bollinger Band Breakout (BBO) strategy.

Back in the late 90's I took the basics of the strategy from Ken Fitschen's well-known Aberration Trading System. Aberration has been named 'One of the Top 10 Trading Systems of All Time' by Futures Truth and remains a popular trading strategy for commodity trend following.

After trading the BBO with futures until 2001 I redesigned the strategy to trade long-only equities. I continue to trade a 'tricked up' version today (called the Growth Portfolio within The Chartist membership offerings) to manage some of our retirement funds.

The rules of the BBO strategy are straightforward:

- ☐ Set the upper Bollinger Band to 3-standard deviations and the lower band to 1-standard deviation.
- ☐ Set the moving average period to 100-days.
- ☐ When the market closes above the upper band, buy on the following day's open.
- ☐ When price closes below the lower band, exit the position on the next day's open.

We'll allocate 5% of capital to each position to create a portfolio of 20 positions. As usual commissions have been included.

The following chart shows the equity growth of the strategy since 2010 through to today vs Buy & Hold.

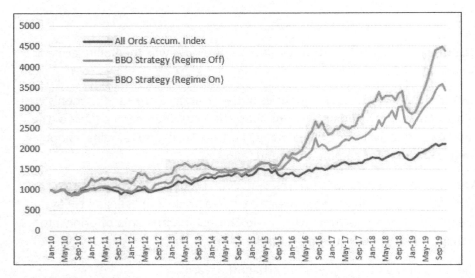

As per the book, and my own trading, I have also plotted the equity growth of the same system using an Index or Regime Filter.

A Regime Filter will only allow new positions to be entered when the broader market trend is up. If the broader market trend is down, we do not take any new positions.

The Regime Filter hasn't added a great deal of benefit in the last 10-years, but as we saw in 2008, it certainly did come in handy by cutting the drawdown substantially.

10-years of out-of-sample data and the BBO continues to show solid returns. This strategy is perfect for an active investor wanting to take control of their capital using a robust approach.

Trend Following on a Weekly Timeframe

One of the most popular systems I wrote about in my 2012 book, Unholy Grails, was the Bollinger Band Breakout strategy (BBO).

That version used daily bars, but a common question I got was, *"How does it perform on weekly data?"*

Back then I coded up a weekly version to appease readers, so let's revisit to see how it's stood up over the last 7-years. We'll call it the Weekly BBO.

In layman's terms the rules are:

When the broader market is in an uptrend, look to buy any stock that breaches the upper side of its Bollinger Band. Place an initial stop 20% below and continue to trail that stop 20% behind as price moves higher. However, if the broader market trend turns down, then tighten that trailing stop to 10%. We will also exit if the stock closes below its lower Bollinger Band.

This strategy uses a slightly tweaked version of the classic Bollinger Band. The specifics are beyond the scope of this article, suffice to say it really won't make a big difference to the bottom line.

Here's how it looks on the chart. We got an entry at $2.19 in early 2012 then an exit in late 2018 at $5.19.

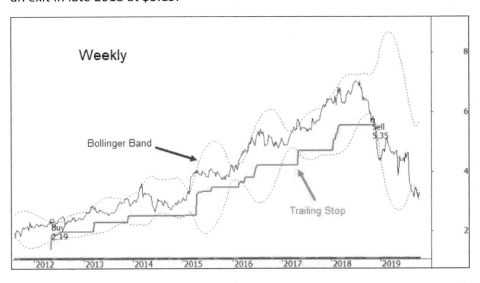

The adaptive trailing stop plays a crucial role.

My research suggests that during broader market selloffs, market leaders tend to consolidate rather than decline. And when that selloff has completed, it's those leaders that head the pack higher.

Giving the position some room to move allows those leaders to consolidate. In other words, I want to keep the "opportunity door" open a little, rather than slam it shut when the market turns down.

The specific rules for this trend strategy are:

1. Define the upward trend of the broader market (in this case the All Ordinaries Index - XAO) using a 10-week simple moving average. If the market is above that average, then it's deemed to be bullish, and we'll take new positions. Below is bearish so no new positions.

2. To the universe of stocks add a 40-week Bollinger Band calibrated to 3-standard deviations.

3. Entry: If a stock closes above the upper band on a Friday, then buy the open on the following Monday. Do not act during the week. Also note, I want the first close above the band only as the signal. There are times where the liquidity filter or the regime filter meets their criteria after the higher close. Ignore these.

4. Exit 1: If the stock declines and closes for the week >=20% from the prior close, exit the position on the next weekly open.

5. Exit 2: If the broader market trend turns down, i.e., the close of the XAO is below the 10-week simple moving average, then exit the position on the next weekly open if price has fallen >= 10% from its highest close. This is the adaptive stop loss at work.

6. Exit 3: Exit the position if the weekly close is below the lower Bollinger Band. This rule rarely plays a part in the system.

Let's now put the theory to the test using the following assumptions:

Universe: ASX All Ordinaries Index + historical constituents (2020 symbols).
Range: January 1999 - October 2019.

Comm's: $6 or 0.08% whichever is higher.
Dividends: Included.
Interest: Excluded.
Liquidity: Volume > 500,000 average for last 5-days and cannot exceed 10% of days total volume.
Position: 20 positions of 5% account value.

Here's the equity growth chart:

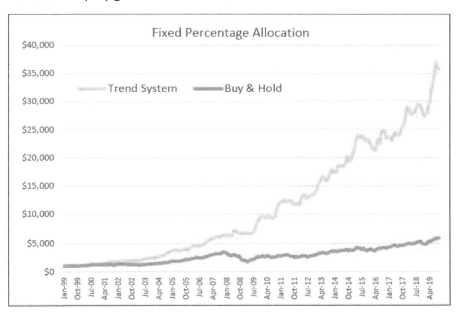

Performance capsule:

CAGR: 18.6% (Buy and hold = 8.8%)
MaxDD: -13.8%
Trades: 661
Win%:   56.3%
W/L Ratio: 2.13
PFactor: 2.74
Win Months: 67.2%
Loss Years: 2 (2011, 2018)

The strategy has continued its strong performance on out-of-sample data over the last 7-years. Whilst one of those years posted a loss, four posted returns above 19%.

The low drawdown comes from two elements. Firstly, the regime filter of 10-weeks is very tight which enables the system to switch off quickly. Secondly, the adaptive stop also allows open profits to be protected when a market decline takes shape.

So why use 40-weeks for the Bollinger Band?

I have no idea where I got that from. Below is the return profile of every parameter between 10 weeks and 100 weeks that suggests the length of the lookback is negligible and it's very robust.

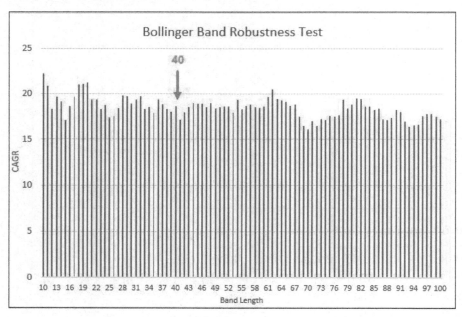

Hedging Portfolio Exposure

A hedge is designed to protect a portfolio from adverse market movements.

As I trade four long-only trend following portfolios, I want to protect from sudden and large downside shifts in the broader market, especially if there is some type of upcoming event. Plus, all being active portfolios I'd only use the hedge whilst the positions remain open.

Common ways to hedge a portfolio include:

- exiting partial positions
- buying put options
- buying a reverse ETF
- initiating a collar with options
- shorting index futures

Be aware that some of these can be complex (collars), can be costly (puts), can deviate from the underlying benchmark (reverse ETFs) or provide excessive exposure (futures).

If you are considering hedging, the selected hedge should be aligned with your knowledge and account size.

Also, it's important that the hedge doesn't morph into its own trading system.

I'm only interested in large moves. Attempting to iron out every crease will be a costly and frustrating exercise. I'm more inclined to let the cards fall where they may, rather than hedge, but then again, my (trading) psychological fortitude is a lot higher than most.

Personally, I prefer to use index futures, namely the Nasdaq-100 Emini for US portfolios and AUD (Australian Dollar) futures for currency exposure. They are aligned with the portfolio holdings, easy to access via the same platform and, being leveraged, are cheap to hold and trade.

To calculate the correct hedge for a long-only equity portfolio, I calculate the beta of the portfolio. Beta refers to the movement of the underlying shares compared to the underlying index. In this case I will use Nasdaq-100 Emini futures as my base index. A stock with a beta of 1.0 will move up and down in sync with the index. A stock with a beta of 0.5 will move half the distance of the index and a 2.0 beta means a movement in the share price twice that of the index.

The following table assumes a portfolio value of $200,000. I calculate the beta of each position against the index. In this example the average beta for the portfolio is 1.03, which is surprisingly low. During high volatility periods, such as October 2019 the beta was closer to 1.6.

I then multiply the portfolio value by the beta. This is essentially saying that for every movement in the Nasdaq-100 futures the portfolio will roughly move the same amount.

	Beta	Close	# Shares	Value
			Portfolio Value	200,000
ES_NQ	1	7267	1	145,340
XLNX	1.41	122.48	327	40,000
WDAY	0.53	187.04	214	40,000
MELI	1.95	493.79	81	40,000
CDNS	0.47	61.16	654	40,000
LULU	0.78	144.18	277	40,000
Avg Beta	1.03			205,600
			Hedge Ratio	71%

Next, we calculate how many index futures will be required to protect the portfolio. The following table highlights the underlying value of the Nasdaq-100 Emini contract. That value is $20 times the current price, which puts a single contract value at $145,340.

For smaller accounts there is a Micro Emini contract with a value of $2 times the underlying index.

Remember the goal of the hedge is not to make a profit; it's to protect the position.

So, in this example if I hedge using a single contract then I will protect about 71% of the value of the portfolio, and for the most part that's enough, or I could revert to the Micro contracts.

	Beta	Close	# Shares	Value
Portfolio Value				**200,000**
ES_NQ	1	7267	1	145,340
XLNX	1.41	122.48	327	40,000
WDAY	0.53	187.04	214	40,000
MELI	1.95	493.79	81	40,000
CDNS	0.47	61.16	654	40,000
LULU	0.78	144.18	277	40,000
Avg Beta	1.03			205,600
Hedge Ratio				**71%**

When to hedge?

As stated above, as a rule I'm wary of attempting to hedge against every downside blip, but obviously a downside blip can turn nasty very quickly.

To date I have not managed to create a systematic way to manage this process.

52-Week High Rotation Strategy

Our research regime centres around improving current systems and ensuring they're synced to the current market environment.

We also spend time looking at new ideas that can either stand on their own or be used in conjunction with other systems.

The following is an adaptation of a strategy that came across my desk. Here's how it works:

1. The S&P 500 must be above the 200-day moving average.
2. Measure the market for stocks within 10% of their 52-week highs.
3. Rank those by percentage distance from that high point (to 5 decimal places).
4. Buy the top 5 and hold for one month.
5. Repeat the following month.

The important rule here is that candidates can only be within 10% of their 52-week high. If not, they're not included.

Here's the equity growth vs. Buy & Hold (including commissions, excluding dividends and interest).

From 2003 through 2015 the strategy generated a return of +13.5% vs the benchmark return of +6.88%.

Drawdown was half that of the index and the 200-day filter allowed the strategy to perform admirably during the 2008 crisis.

However, and interestingly, since 2015 the strategy has failed to keep pace with the underlying index and is currently in a -14% drawdown.

What we've outlined here is a good starting point to building an active strategy to beat the market, protect capital during sustained downswings and without much workload.

World Stock Market Rotation Strategy

We've investigated buying a portfolio of weak stocks vs buying strong stocks on an annual basis, specifically buying the strongest (weakest) for the year, holding for the following year, then repeating.

What we found is a lot can go wrong with an already struggling company in the space of a year.

What about a country ETF?

In this exercise we'll measure the momentum of 42 country ETFs for the prior year then rank from strongest to weakest. We'll then buy the strongest (weakest), hold for 1-year, then repeat^.

This first chart, extending back to 1997, shows the return if we invested 100% into the strongest country ETF.

And this next chart shows the return the following year if we bought the weakest country ETF from the prior year.

But what happens when we put each return profile together?

The following chart offers some interesting insights. Buying the strongest country ETF worked extremely well until the financial crisis. The strategy caught 5-years of large upside moves culminating in a 50% gain in China through 2007.

That China gain was promptly crushed through 2008. Since then, buying the prior winner has failed to hold itself together. Indeed, there are several instances where the prior best performer becomes the worst performer the following year.

For the contrarians, buying the prior worst performer has been a reasonably steady strategy and has outperformed the S&P 500 by about 50%.

Regardless of the S&P 500 outperformance it's been a very lumpy ride and not one I'd personally undertake. As stated above, this exercise corroborates the theory that a lot can go wrong in the space of a year.

I'll stick to being an active investor.

Trading and Hindsight Bias

"Had you invested $1 in XYZ in 1943 it would now be worth $1.9 billion".

I knew it was a good investment!

The problem is we didn't know it all along, we only feel as though we did.

That's hindsight bias.

Another typical example came across my desk recently. To quote the article[2], "Apple is one of the top performing stocks of the past 27 years with a +11,393% return but what if I told you there was a trend trading signal that doubled those returns to +25,896%? Would you be interested?"

The secret sauce?

"This trend trading strategy signals to go long when the 10-day EMA crosses and closes over the 50-day EMA and to go back to cash when the 10-day EMA crosses under and closes below the 50-day EMA."

The following chart offers the equity growth of $1000 with all profits reinvested. I have used commissions, including stock splits and dividends.

---

[2] https://www.newtraderu.com/2019/10/18/the-best-aapl-price-action-trading-strategy/

Not quite the double performance as suggested in the article but the strategy does outperform buy and hold. However, we're discussing hindsight bias rather than performance metrics.

The obvious question is why use Apple as an example in the first place?

Back in 2000, while Apple was still in nappies, Sun Microsystems (JAVA) was Silicon Valley's most prominent company and one of IT's great innovators. Even today, employees and management still talk about the great work being done at Sun Microsystems.

Applying the EMA crossover rules to JAVA as at January 2000 leaves AAPL in the dust. Why would you choose AAPL and not JAVA to continue the strategy with?

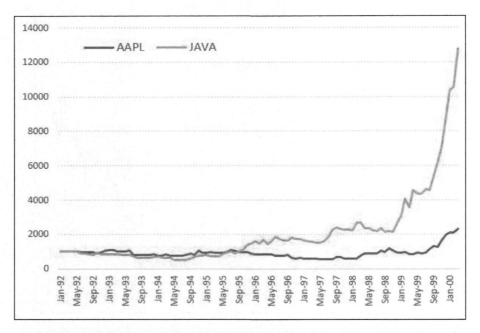

Because JAVA fell some 97% during the Tech crash, and continued lower until it was finally purchased by Oracle in 2010. In other words it didn't survive, but AAPL did.

That's hindsight bias.

So how do we know if AAPL will keep on keeping on? Or will it become the next JAVA?

Does the 10/50 EMA crossover strategy have broader merit as a strategy?

The conclusion?

We can't know what the future holds for a single stock. Basing a strategy on an individual stock that has been cherry-picked from past performance is risky. Stocks, and even markets, change personalities over time, therefore cherry-picked strategies will fail.

The solution is to better understand the robustness of the strategy itself. To do that it should be tested over a larger universe of symbols.

I'll run a basic test across every stock in the S&P 500. Each position will be allocated $1000, and every possible trade taken. The idea being to see how the strategy performs across many individual stocks.

S&P 500 Constiuents (1999 - Today)	
# Wins	406
Win %	81.2%
Avg Win	1696
Avg Loss	-409
W/L Ratio	4.15
Profit Factor	17.4

These figures are impressive.

406 (81%) constituents show a profit after 20-years of trading. The average winning stock makes over 4 times the average losing stock.

The following table shows that AAPL is not the most profitable during the period. It comes in at number 5.

Top 5 Performers ($)	
QCOM	12958
NFLX	11507
NVDA	9058
MNST	8779
AAPL	7986
Bottom 5 Performers ($)	
BK	-1020
BMY	-1215
LLY	-1251
XLNX	-1300
CTL	-1448

So, what's the problem with the strategy? It certainly looks appealing when we view it through this lens.

Here's the thing...

As of November 2019 there are 314 possible positions within the S&P 500 universe.

Which ones to take? We know we can't use hindsight to pick the best ones - the personality of individual stocks changes over time.

To test the validity of the strategy itself, we need to rank the potential trades. For this simple exercise we'll use the momentum of the stock over the last 50-days. When faced with more signals than cash available, we'll take the highest ranked signals only.

The portfolio will consist of 20 positions calculated by the ranking and each allocated 5% of equity. Commissions included. Here's the equity growth chart:

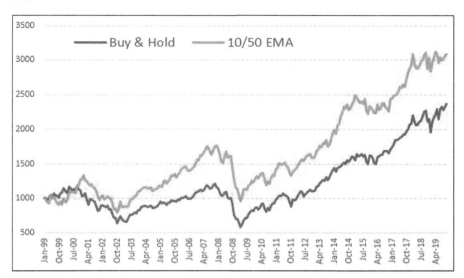

The strategy shows a slight out-performance compared to Buy & Hold. What's not shown is the trade win rate that stands at 32% - extremely low and very difficult for most traders to cope with.

The drawdown during the 2008 crisis was still very steep at 48%. That may improve slightly with a regime filter.

In summary the 10/50 EMA crossover system is not overly compelling when used on a larger universe. Of course, if we could know what the best performing stock in the coming 20-years will be, we'd go all in.

But we can only know that with Hindsight Bias.

Are Two Triggers Better Than One?

A trigger is the reason a trade is made. If X happens, then buy. If Y happens, then sell.

But what if we combined two triggers, would this increase the success of the trade? i.e., if X & Y happen, then buy.

Let's put it to the test.

The two triggers will be a breakout above a 50-day moving average and a MACD crossing above the zero line.

We'll test on 20-years of data using the Russell-1000 + historical constituents. As was established in *Unholy Grails*[3], the use of a regime filter enhances risk adjusted returns, so we'll also use a 200-day average of the S&P 500 to define the broader market trend.

The following table establishes a foundation for both triggers individually using a portfolio of 20 equally weighted positions. The positions are held between 5 and 20 days then exited. No stops or other criteria are used.

50-day SMA Breakout

	Hold Time (Days)				Buy &
	5	10	15	20	Hold
CAGR	8.5%	10.5%	10.6%	10.3%	4.7%
Win%	52.2%	53.5%	54.3%	54.9%	100%
W/L Ratio	1.03	1.05	1.03	1.1	n/a
maxDD	-24.8%	-24.3%	-28.6%	-22.0%	-56.8%

MACD Cross

	Hold Time (Days)				Buy &
	5	10	15	20	Hold
CAGR	7.6%	9.1%	9.4%	7.1%	4.7%
Win%	52.1%	53.5%	55.5%	54.6%	100%
W/L Ratio	1.04	1.01	0.96	1.01	n/a
maxDD	-22.2%	-24.8%	-26.7%	-25.9%	-56.8%

---

[3] Radge, N. (2012) *Unholy Grails – A New Road to Wealth*, Australia, Radge Publishing

Both triggers show a win rate slightly better than random. The win rates rise slightly as the hold period lengthens which is more a function of the markets upward bias.

The next table shows the results when the two triggers are combined. To generate a buy signal, price must move above the 50-day SMA and the MACD zero line and these must occur within 5 days of each other.

Dual Signals

	Hold Time (Days)				Buy &
	5	10	15	20	Hold
CAGR	7.0%	8.4%	8.4%	6.8%	4.7%
Win%	51.9%	53.5%	55.0%	54.2%	100%
W/L Ratio	1.04	1.00	0.97	1.21	n/a
maxDD	-27.9%	-27.2%	-25.6%	-26.1%	-56.8%

The evidence suggests combining these two signals doesn't increase success. Indeed, the metrics deteriorate slightly across the board.

There are a myriad of trigger types and there is scope that a combination of the right two could produce a better outcome than what's been presented here.

The bottom line is every theory or strategy should be thoroughly tested to truly understand its merits.

Revisiting My First Trading System

Let's spin the clock back to 1985.

Trading fell in my lap one day. Randomly. One of those life changing events.

The strategy wasn't mine, yet I could see trends and thus profits.

The rules?

Buy when the 5-day moving average crossed above the 10-day. Sell when the 5-day crossed back down through the 10-day.

That was it. No position sizing. No stop losses. Nothing.

I know...I know. I shudder at the thought too.

I traded a single contract in the Share Price Index Futures from late 1985 through early 1987. Here are some stats that I have attempted to recreate from memory:

Total Return: +90.7%
CAGR: +53.8%
maxDD: -15.2%
Trades: 36
Win%:   41%
W/L ratio: 2.6

And here's the equity curve for the period.

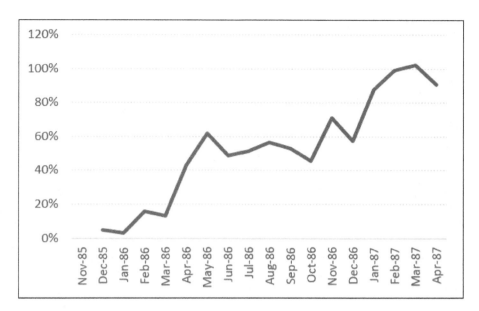

A 90% return in some 15-months.

No skill here. Pure luck. The adage "Don't confuse brilliance with a bull market" comes to mind. Let's remember that the run from 1982 to the 1987 high was one of the strongest bull markets for decades.

I ceased trading the strategy in early 1987, shown at "A" on the chart below. The reason is a story for another time, albeit driven by ego and greed.

Needless to say, the strategy went short on September 28th, 1987 and collected a 300% windfall on the Black Monday crash (shown at "B"). I wasn't involved. Ironically, the strategy I switched to blew up and my father bailed me out.

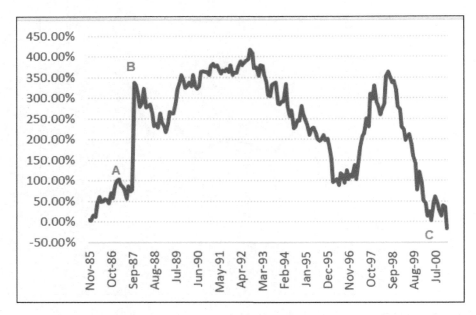

Over the next few years, the strategy continued to make new highs before declining to terminal ruin in mid 2000 (shown at "C").

Long term followers know I'm a big believer in understanding why a strategy makes money. Doing so enables us to gain more insight to understand how or why a strategy could fail.

Or in this case how terminal ruin came about.

Over the longer term the strategy showed standard trend following metrics; a win rate in the 40% - 45% range, and a win/loss ratio around 2.5 to 3.0.

So, what went wrong?

Two attributes contributed to the rapid decline.

To start with the average loss was -13.7% of account value. Compare that to today where my average loss is -0.57%. Even the worst loss in recent memory for me is -1.98%.

That can work when the market is being kind as it seemed to do when I was trading the strategy. But if you trade long enough, you'll soon realise the market can get a little cranky at times.

Modeling suggests a strategy with a win rate of 41% has a probability of 12 losing trades in a row.

Which is exactly what occurred between 1999 to 2000.

And when each loss represents nearly 14% of account value, the risk of ruin is 100%.

In summary, it was just a matter of time.

An Effective Mean Reversion System

This chapter is an excerpt from the Trading System Mentor Course[4].

Mean reversion is the process of prices moving away from the respective average or mean price and then reverting, in some instances quite quickly.

Mean reversion is the opposite of momentum.

Momentum relies on the long tails that sustained trends provide and the goal is to ride those trends for as long as possible.

Mean reversion, on the other hand, relies on choppy random price action and preferably tight price tails so that price snaps back very quickly.

If we review a trade distribution chart we can see where the two strategies generate their respective profits. Mean reversion operates in the 'noise' where most trades take place, whereas Momentum operates in the 'outlier' areas where not many trades occur.

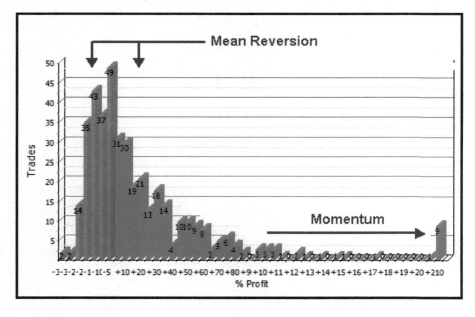

---

[4] https://nickradge.com/mentor-course

There is significant evidence to suggest that markets trend just 30% of the time, and therefore are directionless the other 70%.

Even in a stock market, which tends to have a long-term upside bias, price action tends to be quite random. Over the last 10-years 1338 (52.9%) days were up and 1187 (46.9%) were down.

The following chart of Commonwealth Bank (CBA.au) shows typical stock price action - rotation back and forth for 12-months before starting to trend.

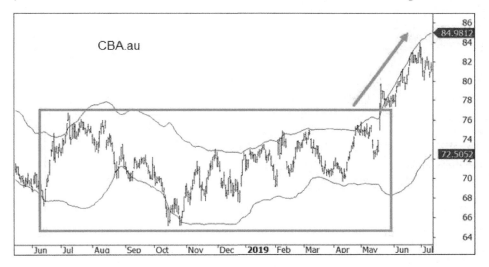

The blue lines shown in the chart above are Bollinger Bands which calculate the standard deviation around a mean price. Price excursions beyond the bands tend to be reversed most of the time and they therefore lend themselves to be a good tool as a starting foundation.

Another popular method of identifying reversal points is an overbought/oversold oscillator such as a Relative Strength Index (RSI), shown on the chart below. In this example the trades are shorter in time frame rather than the above example which is looking for extended swings back and forth.

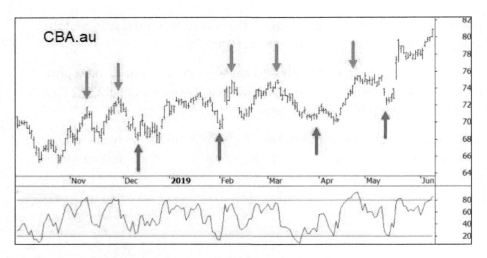

Mean reversion strategies are popular because they tend to have a high win rate and a faster feedback loop.

Another popular trait of Mean Reversion strategies is that the Maximum Wait reading, or time to recover from an equity decline, is low. This means the strategy tends to pull itself out of a drawdown quicker than a momentum strategy.

Here are the rules.

In layman's terms the rules are:

When a stock is trending higher, look for a heavily oversold point. Once an oversold level is attained, place a buy order below the market for the following day. If that order is filled, await the first higher close then exit the position on the next open.

Here's how it looks...

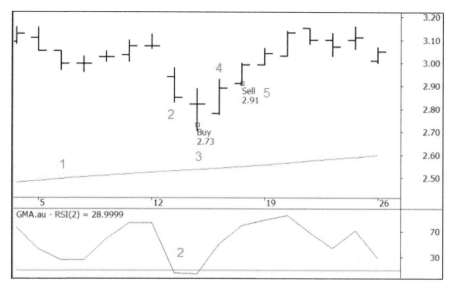

GMA.au - RSI(2) = 28.9999

1. Define the upward trend of the stock using a 100-day simple moving average. If the stock is above that average, then it's deemed to be bullish.

2. Look for a pullback in that trend using a 2-day RSI. When that falls below 10, the stock is considered heavily oversold.

3. Rank any candidates using Rate of Change and select the top 5.

4. Calculate the Average True Range (ATR) for the prior 10 days. Subtract this from the current low and place a LIMIT buy order at that level for tomorrow. This is known as the 'stretch'.

5. If the LIMIT buy level is met, then wait for the first higher close.

6. Exit the position on the following open.

Let's now put the theory to the test using the following assumptions:

Universe: ASX All Ordinaries Index + historical constituents (2020 symbols).

Range: January 1999 - September 2019.
Comm's: $6 or 0.08% whichever is higher.
Dividends: Excluded.
Interest: Excluded.

Liquidity: Volume > 300,000 average for last 5-days and cannot
                  exceed 10% of days total volume.
Position: 5 positions of 20% account value

Here's the equity growth chart:

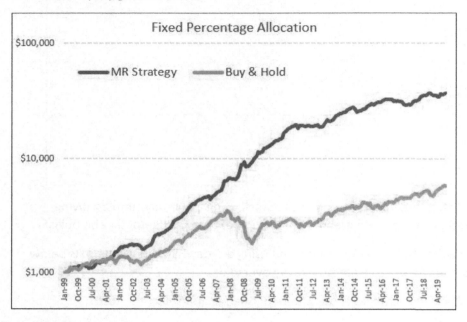

Performance capsule:

CAGR: 19.1% (Buy and hold = 8.8%)
MaxDD: 15.3%
Trades: 1786
Win%:   67.8%
W/L Ratio: 0.96
PFactor: 1.96
Win Months: 75%
Loss Years: 1 (2012)

This Mean Reversion strategy, with minimal rules and linear parameters, has shown some solid results. Drawdowns are in the 13% - 15% range which is palatable.

TRADING PSYCHOLOGY & MOTIVATION

10 Simple Tips that Give me the Trading Edge

A question put to me by a reader made me think long and hard.

He wrote, *"In trading, what qualities are needed to be your best? In other words, why do you succeed where others failed?"*

Well, success is in the eye of the beholder, but I guess I've done okay at mastering a life/work balance.

I have done well for a few reasons.

1. I study. Ever since I walked onto the floor of the stock exchange back in 1985, I was enthralled. I spent every lunch break in the ASX bookstore. Then I found the bookstore at the Sydney Futures Exchange. So, I spent my lunch times there. I still study.

2. I don't just study trading. I study traders. All the greatest traders have had to walk the same journey as us. It's important to understand the context of what you're doing. I study their track records, processes, history – just about anything that catches my eye.

3. I don't just study traders. I read between the lines. When people read a trading book, they see the words but not the true meaning of what is being said. Many times, the valuable lessons are not in the written word. Rather what is being alluded to.

4. I have no fear. The market can't hurt me. Position sizing and diversification see to that.

5. I'm only interested in facts and what is practical and useful. I have always applied a rules-based approach to trading. Left brain bias. Research, problems, and solutions are processed within a structured environment.

6. I make decisions based on good process rather than monetary outcome. I have no attachment to losses or periods of losses. Which means I can continue to follow the process and achieve my objectives.

7. I accept there is much I can't control. I can however control my reactions to events – good and bad. Much of that control comes from having no attachment to the money.

8. I have patience. A moderately good strategy applied over the long term will generate more wealth than chasing the latest fad. The Eighth Wonder of the World is compounding. And compounding requires time to develop.

9. I am consistent. I can place trades every day. Every week. Every month. Every year. Without fail.

10. If all else fails I go fishing. Fishing is my meditation.

The Big Easy

In a remarkable turn of events, I found myself at the golf range (OK, Trish dragged me out).

Alongside me were several international students honing their skills.

When I say students, I don't mean students of golf.

When I say honing their skills, I am being polite.

They certainly weren't physics students. They seemed to be adamant that the harder they swung the club, the further the ball would travel. When this theory didn't achieve the desired results, they tossed out a few expletives in some unknown dialect and let fly with another cruel and violent swipe at the ball.

Reload. Ping. Kinyezi!

Clearly the students didn't understand what the 'sweet spot' was designed for. The sweet spot on the head of a golf club delivers the most energy to the ball to launch it farther and straighter.

A mild and measured half swing delivered with minimal effort will send a golf ball a lot straighter and a lot further than a fully-fledged assault.

Trading and investing are similar.

The harder you try, the worse off you generally are.

Watching the screen all day, desperately willing your portfolio higher, hopping in and out like a whack-a-mole day trader or silently praying to the market gods is not about being in the sweet spot.

They call Ernie Els 'The Big Easy' because he's big and he swings it easy. His career results are a testament to finding the sweet spot.

As your trading caddy I recommend the same.

One Simple Step to Avoid Financial disaster

There is one element that determines whether you will be a successful trader or a failure.

Completion of a trade will determine your success.

Exiting positions makes the world of difference.

Anyone can buy a stock, and they do, but most people don't finish. Finishing things – exiting a position – is what makes progress.

If you close a losing trade, for example, it's finished. You're free of it, your mind is free and you can move onto the next one.

But if you have too many trades open, ones that you don't know how to finish, that are keeping your brain, your emotions and your resources occupied, you're never really going to make any progress.

The key to success is in the planning. You want to know before you enter a trade exactly how and when you plan to exit. You want to know the end goal, when a trade is finished; good or bad.

Knowing what the finish point looks like makes trading goals easier to achieve.

A lot of people want to know what a company does, what they produce, what their financials are like, the management track record and the prospects in that sector. All of this is important, but it doesn't tell you where the finish line is. And since trade completion is what separates successful traders from perpetual failures, shouldn't you start thinking about every position you take in terms of exiting?

What does the finish line look like?

Your brain is wired to make you hang onto trades that are working against you. Does your brain tell you "Hang on, the stock price will turn around! It will come good...eventually." Or "what goes down must come back up again...one day." Some big names in Australia failed to recover. HIH didn't come back up. OneTel didn't come back up and neither did ABC Learning.

Are you hanging onto a plunging stock waiting for it to turn around? Who knows how long that could take or if it will turn around? No one, that's who.

Understanding the optimal level to maximise profit yet minimise loss is what separates successful traders from the rest.

Talent is a small and inconsequential factor compared to executing and finishing a trade. Completion is the #1 thing most people are missing.

Create a trading plan with rules outlining exactly how you will enter a trade, and more importantly, how and when you will exit. In your plan set out exactly how many positions you will hold at any one time.

A simple way we recommend members of The Chartist's Growth Portfolio manage their positions is to divide their capital into 10 equal parts. Ten stocks is manageable and not overwhelming. If you have a smaller account, say under $20,000, then you may want to reduce that number to avoid commission drag.

Set yourself a simple routine each day; check if your stocks have hit your exit criteria. If they have, close the position immediately and enjoy the process of choosing the next stock to buy.

Keep a trading diary; write down how you felt when you bought or sold, what was going through your mind? Did you stick to your plan? If not, why not? If you find you are over-riding your plan often, then it's time to stop and make some changes or seek help from a trusted advisor.

Defining your exit criteria will help improve your trading results and will boost your confidence as a trader.

Patience is the Key to Trading Success

New traders often expect instant success, focusing on the easy money. We hear the stories of people that have made a lot of money, quickly. Bitcoin comes to mind.

Generally, this success is based on pure luck.

It's a natural human desire to focus on success. We want to be lucky. It's like buying a lottery ticket. We read about the person who wins twenty-five million dollars but fail to acknowledge the other four hundred and eighty thousand people that lost their money on the same bet.

It's the same with golf. We see Jason Day, Jordan Spieth and Rory McIlroy's success but what we don't see is the other twenty-five thousand players slugging it out, sleeping in the back of cars, trying to make some coin as a professional golfer.

Making money trading may not happen next week, maybe not next month, and maybe not next year... but it's going to happen eventually.

The goal in your first year is twofold. Firstly, not to blow your capital. That's a significant goal. Continuing the golf analogy, try to keep the ball on the fairway. Don't worry about trying to shoot a par or a birdie. Just keep the ball on the fairway so you stay in the game.

The second goal is to allow the trades to unfold. You can't control the market. The want or the need to look at prices during the day is nothing more than you willing the market in your direction. You can put a steak on a barbeque but you can't will it to cook. It's going to cook in its own time. It's the same with trading. You can look at the price as much as you want but that's not going to make it move.

If you understand that your strategy has a mathematical edge, and that it will work over the long term, then there's no need to be watching the price during the day. Allow the trade to unfold and follow your plan.

Let's Talk Percentages

I often receive emails or phone calls from people saying,

"Help! My trading account is down $5000, and I don't know what to do." It's usually followed by "My partner is going to kill me."

My first response is "Let's take a step back. What's your account size and what percentage does the $5000 represent?"

There are two reasons why we shouldn't talk in dollar terms.

Firstly, dollars do not equalise account fluctuations. There is a big difference between a $5000 loss on a $10,000 account (50%) and a $5000 loss on a $100,000 account (5%). You don't hear fund managers talking in dollar terms – they speak in percentages because it enables a direct comparison.

Secondly, speaking in dollar terms makes losses more personal and more emotional. We tend to relate dollar losses with an hourly work rate to recover the loss. A $5000 trading loss may mean 2-weeks on the job to recoup.

Having that psychological weight only adds to the pressure. And as we know with many things in life, the harder you try, the harder it becomes.

Instead, aim for an almost 'blasé' state of mind or a position where individual losses do not make a material difference to your mindset.

To do this, only trade with money you can afford to lose.

Not wanting to lose money is a type of anchoring bias.

It results in bad positions being held in the hope that the trade will at least revert to breakeven at some stage. That focus ensures you ignore all other information that may be more important to the decision-making process. You are anchored to the poor decision (hanging on to a bad trade).

In late 2015 Dick Smith Holdings (DSH) dropped some 85%. Rather than say SELL many brokers downgraded their recommendations from BUY to HOLD.

Hold for what?

These brokers are anchoring their opinion on other information to save face. The fact that the stock was at $2.20 earlier in the year, yet is now $0.20, is ignored.

Dick Smith Holdings collapsed in 2016 with shareholders losing all their money.

Opportunity cost is a large expense that is overlooked by most of the financial services industry.

The George Costanza School of Trading

Have you ever watched *'Seinfeld'*?

Cracks me up whenever I watch it.

A favourite is the episode where George Costanza does everything in opposites.

He saw an attractive woman in the diner, walked up to her and, instead of lying and conning her into a date, said he was a short, bald, unemployed man who still lives with his parents.

She immediately went out with him.

Then, he gets a job interview with the New York Yankees.

Instead of sucking up to the owner he tells him how much the team sucks and why every decision is stupid.

He gets the job.

So what's the point?

Every time George did the opposite to what he would normally do, what logic and common sense dictates him do, he 'won'.

It's the same for trading and investing and the stock market.

Why?

Firstly, consider that most retail investors perform badly (research from Blackrock shows the average investor has returned 2.1% over the last 20-years compared to the market return of 7.8%).

It could easily be assumed that most people are making the same, albeit broad, investment decisions.

Therefore, if most people are making the same decisions most of the time, it's not a large leap to assume they're also making what is obviously a 'logical' or 'common sense' decision – probably the first one that pops into their mind.

Which immediately suggests that a logical, common-sense decision or reaction that initially comes to mind must be the wrong one.

It certainly can't be the right one – the data would suggest otherwise.

How about the stock market itself, specifically the US stock market?

Many have said the country is an economic wasteland. It's bankrupt, the fiscal cliff, rising debt, rising unemployment, out of control trade deficits, asset sales and who knows what else? It's an economic disaster and for the last 10-years the doomsayers have told you to stock up on baked beans and gold.

Yet, throughout all this, the US stock market continued to hit all-time highs. Not just the Dow Jones, but the S&P 500 and all the way down through the ranks to the Russell 2000. It's a real broad-based bull market.

In 1936, during the darkest day of the depression when US unemployment was running at 18%, the Dow Jones rose 24%.

Where is the logic?

And how is that gold trade everyone has been ranting about for over 10-years? Buy gold, buy gold, buy gold!

What's been one of the worst investments over the last 10-years (2011 – 2020)?

Gold.

Where is the logic?

Which is exactly my point.

Logic has absolutely nothing to do with it.

Often the first reaction you have to an investment situation, especially under duress, is the incorrect decision.

So next time you're faced with a difficult investment decision, ask yourself, "What would George Costanza do?"

DIY Brazilian

In the early 90's I spent 4 years on the trading floor of the Sydney Futures Exchange – yes, the place with hundreds of overpaid, testosterone overloaded 20-somethings who spent their day screaming and shouting whilst flashing strange hand gestures at each other. At 23 I was in my element. On the surface it appeared a great job

The problem was that every 15 minutes of pure adrenaline was punctuated by full days of complete boredom.

What do 300 bored and brash 20-somethings do when they have to stand around for days on end when trading was quiet?

We flew paper planes, played pin-the-tail on the visitor's butt, enjoyed long, expensive lunches and lots of bluster and banter. It was, after all, the halcyon days of the 90's and we were a bunch of 'bankers'.

It was during this banter, and highly likely after a long lunch, that the topic of the Brazilian came up.

But not the variety you're thinking of.

The Brazilian trade.

The Brazilian trade is one that's impossible to lose on. It really is the Holy Grail. Imagine taking a trade and you knew that you couldn't lose?

Let's step through the trade.

[At this point I need you to remind you to read the disclaimer at the start of this book – the one about "Past results are not indicative of future performance…". I can't be held responsible for the outcome of this trade should you wish to take it.]

Here we go – the Brazilian trade. The no-loss, Holy Grail of trades.

Step 1

You need to enter an eye-poppingly large position in a very volatile futures contract. Back in the day we always used the S&P 500 futures, but today you could also use the Hang Seng or Nikkei 225. It doesn't matter whether it's a long or short position – you know my thoughts about prediction. Just take a position but it must be a 'Nick Leeson size' position. The bigger, the better. Ideally you put this trade on right before a significant economic news release, something like the US Non-Farm Payrolls, or any other event that tends to send the market into a frenzy.

Step 2

Once you have initiated the position, take a walk down to the local Flight Centre office and book a one-way First-Class ticket to Rio de Janeiro in Brazil (or any other non-extradition country). Now the agent will try to sell you a return ticket – that's their job after all – but politely refuse and stick to the plan (Plan the trade, trade the plan).

Step 3

Wait for said major economic release.

There are two possible outcomes.

The first is the market moves in the right direction for your position. You become an instant multi-millionaire and spend the rest of your life with bragging rights. Ideally you should never make another trade.

The other outcome is the market moves the wrong way, but this too is okay. Take a cab to the airport with your passport and one-way First-Class ticket and sit back knowing you'll spend the rest of your life strolling along Copacabana Beach. You may need to get a job pouring beers or washing plates, but who'd complain? You're in paradise.

Now you probably think I'm pulling your chain – but I'm not. A Goldman Sachs trader pleaded guilty to a scheme hiding an $8 billion trade in the S&P 500 futures[5]. $8 billion – whoa! That really is 'Nick Leeson big'.

Problem is technically this wasn't a Brazilian trade because he only made the trade and didn't book the ticket. In this case it's really a Retirement Trade

---

[5] https://www.justice.gov/usao-sdny/pr/former-goldman-sachs-vice-president-sentenced-manhattan-federal-court-nine-months

instead. The risk with a Retirement Trade is that it goes from the wanted 'no loss' Brazilian trade to a 50/50 win/loss bet – and usually you'll get the wrong side of the coin. When that happens, you tend to go to jail like the Goldman Sachs guy, or you'll be doing plenty of extra work paying back the margin call from your broker.

So, what's the point of this story?

One day you will have a Retirement trade come your way. It may have already been dangled in front of you.

Yes, THE big one.

One came my way back in 1999 (I was only slightly more mature than the trading floor days).

I got a call from a close friend who shall remain nameless as he may read this book. He was sure a certain company was going to be the 'next big thing'.

So, I placed a Retirement Trade.

The big one.

The one that would set me up for life. Not illegal but it was big.

And yes, it went badly wrong.

To this day it remains the largest loss I've had by far.

So, when you dream up your own Retirement Trade, or when you get approached by a trusted friend with the 'no loss' proposition, once again ask yourself...

"What would George Costanza do?"

Bringing Down the House

Many years ago (pre-children) Trish and I took a holiday to the Gold Coast. After setting ourselves up in a nice apartment overlooking the beach for a week of sun and R&R, we decided to make a trip to Jupiters Casino for dinner at one of the mid-tier eateries and enjoy a bit of razzle-dazzle.

After dinner the tables beckoned and let's face it, so long as I refrained from using weird hand gestures there wasn't a great leap from the trading floor to the casino table – both are noisy, encourage punters and distribute wealth from one party to another.

And I, of course, had a system.

On that first night (now you know where this is going) the system did well. We not only paid for dinner but the airline tickets.

The following evening, we made the same pilgrimage, ate at the same restaurant, and visited the same table. This time we paid for the full holiday and then some.

The system was on fire.

On the third night (now it's getting sad) we were welcomed back to the casino but this time we ate at the best restaurant and then returned to the same table.

People started taking notice. We were doing the opposite of everyone else. We got a few strange looks. We even got approached by other punters.

"What are you doing?" they'd ask.

"I have a system". Impressive.

We went 6 nights in a row. We won every night. Other punters started copying us. Even the croupiers eyed us off.

We were consistent winners. Six nights in a row. We had no life, but we had a 'system'.

But here's the thing – every night the casino let us back in. We were not met at the door by a 6'6" 150kg bruiser with, "Sorry Mr. & Mrs. Radge. You can't come in tonight."

The casino allows anyone and everyone to play. Winners. Losers. Radges. Even the Packers get a go.

Why?

Because they, The House, have an edge. A clearly defined mathematical edge.

They don't bother to pick and choose who plays. Rather, their core business is to exploit The House's edge and to do that they must accept all-comers and then allow the cards to fall where they may (pun intended).

And the winner is The House. They're big, rich, and glamorous.

Yet the irony is when we trade or invest our own money, we do the opposite. We focus on selecting stocks. The next hot stock. The next hot sector. The next winner. We only want the good ones to come through the door and prefer the bad ones stay outside.

Instead of trying to pick the next big winner or avoid the next dreaded loser, take the casino route and become The House.

Find an edge. Then exploit it. Often.

Ramping Up the Profits

If you are genuinely interested in improving your trading results let's head back to the casino (metaphorically!).

The casino has another little trick up its sleeve that we can learn from. Previously we've pointed out that the casino lets everyone play – the more people who play the more opportunity the casino has to exploit their mathematical edge.

When you walk into the Sydney Star Casino there is something missing. All the flashy lights, glitz, glamour, and razzamatazz are there. Yet something, or more specifically, someone, is missing.

The croupiers.

There is a distinct lack of them. Sure, there are a few around, but more and more of the games are being operated by computers rather than humans.

Why?

There are two ways to increase profitability; increase your edge (which usually means taking on more risk) or increase the rate of exploiting your edge.

At the casino a computer with credit cards inserted can process the dealing and monetary transactions a lot faster than a croupier can manually. This increases the rate of play which, in turn, increases the frequency at which the casino can exploit its edge. If they have a 5% edge on 50 hands in an hour, they can increase their profit simply by playing more hands in that hour. If the computers can double the number of hands being played each hour, they double the casino's profit.

Croupiers: exit stage left.

When we talk about an edge or positive expectancy in trading, we are referring to the ability of a strategy to make profits. That's always a good starting point – everyone wants to make a profit. However, the extent of those profits is influenced by trade frequency.

I read about a trade setup in Commonwealth Bank which had been profitable every year for 15-years. Sounds great. However, apart from sample size issues, the problem is the setup only makes one trade a year. Nobody is going to get rich making one trade a year, unless they dramatically up the ante and bet the house on it.

Let's consider two strategies, both of which have a positive expectancy.

Strategy-A has a winning percentage of 46% and a W/L ratio of 2.43. Sounds very similar to a nice trend following system, which it is. So, every 100 trades will make 57.78 units of profit. Perfect.

Strategy-B on the other hand has a winning percentage of 64.2% with a W/L ratio of just 1.01. Fits the profile of a short-term system, which it is. For every 100 trades it generates 29.04 units of profit. Hmmm...not so perfect as it's half the profit of Strategy-A.

Which would you choose?

If you chose Strategy-A you may need to know it only makes 50 trades each year, so its units of profit per year is 28.89. Strategy-B on the other hand makes 200 trades per year, meaning its yearly profit is 58.08 units.

The trade frequency of Strategy-B is the driver that makes it twice as profitable as Strategy-A in any given year.

Imagine if you could take Strategy-B up to 400 trades a year?

Profits double again.

800?

Food for thought...

Nick Radge

A Tale of An Old Man, A Boy and a Donkey

Have you heard the tale of the old man, the boy, and their donkey?

An old man, a boy and a donkey were going to town. The boy rode on the donkey and the old man walked. As they plodded along, they passed some people who remarked it was a shame the old man was walking and the boy was riding. The man and boy thought maybe the critics were right, so they changed positions.

Later, they passed some people who remarked: "What a shame that he makes the little boy walk." So, they decided to both walk.

Soon they passed some more people who thought they were stupid to walk when they had a decent donkey to ride. So, they both rode the donkey.

Now they passed some people that shamed them by saying how awful to put such a load on a poor donkey. The boy and man said they were probably right, so they decided to carry the donkey. As they crossed the bridge, they lost their grip on the animal who fell into the river and drowned.

The moral of the story?

There are a few that are relevant to trading and investing but I want to focus on one.

You see, everyone has their own perspective.

We all swim in our own pool of logic.

This is a good thing because if we all mirrored each other it would be a boring old world to live in. And nobody would make money.

However, issues arise when we are swayed by too many perspectives from too many people. It sucks us into the Beginners Cycle. It lures us away from what we set out to do. It confuses, complicates, and distracts.

You lose confidence. You lose money.

In trading, if you try to do everything, you might as well... kiss your ass good-bye.

Instead, become good at one thing. Trading one specific pattern. Following a single proven system. Trading a trend. Anything.

But importantly just make it one thing. Do it well. Do it long enough so you become proficient in it.

And turn off all the other noise and chatter.

When you become good at that one method, when it becomes second nature and you thoroughly enjoy the experience of using it and profiting from it, only then should you move to the next strategy.

Questioning Your Hiring and Firing Policies

I've never been in a position to be hiring or firing a lot of people. I come from a background of small teams, although I always knew there was someone above doing the nasty work.

I had a discussion with the owner of a small business that wasn't going too well. He explained that to save money he had put off his highest paid staff, the good staff. Even though I'm not up to date on the latest corporate thinking and trends, I thought this was odd.

During the good times it was these staff that moved the company forward. Outstripping the competition. Setting the pace. Always pushing for, and making, better gains.

And when things got tough, it was these same staff members who put their heads down, bums up, and worked to hold the company together. They waited patiently for things to bounce back when conditions picked up again – which they knew would happen.

But he sacked these ones. And kept the bad ones. The ones who would drag his business down even further.

I had a similar discussion this week with a client who was struggling to manage their 'trading business'.

The fear of the better performing stocks reversing was so great that she sold them and hung onto the poor ones hoping they would miraculously turn around and come good.

Trading is a business. Successful businesses are not based on hope and fear.

Nurture the stocks that are going well. Cut the bad ones.

Hope and fear can easily be overcome by having a plan. A proven trading plan will alleviate anxiety and stress.

The Secret is Not Here...

I'm often asked to list my favourite, most influential trading books. Over the last 35 years I've read a LOT of trading books, good and bad.

Before we go any further let's think...what's in a trading book?

Probably nothing unless you make it your own.

For example, I have known Peter for 15 years. He's a doctor – a specialist, so he must be smart. He loves reading trading books. He has hundreds of them. Whenever a new trading book is released, wham! He ordered it and read it.

He then stows it on a huge bookshelf bulging with trading books.

Like little trophies.

But Peter is not a good trader. In fact, he's given up trading altogether.

If you want to read trading books to collect trophies, that's fine. But if you want to read trading books to enhance your knowledge and become a better trader, then just reading them isn't going to cut it.

You need to act on the knowledge. Run with it. Make it your own.

That is not to say that everything in a trading book is worthwhile, but you need to explore, test, and validate the parts that may enhance your trading arsenal.

So rather than tell you what books I like, I'd like to tell you how certain books influenced me and how I used the information to improve my trading skills.

PPS Trading Strategy by Curtis Arnold

I had been plodding along with my trading until I read this book back in the 90's.

It was the life changer.

The light bulb moment.

It just made sense: low risk patterns, high win/loss ratios, a positive expectancy.

This book was my first serious foray into systems testing and design (I had tinkered during the 80's firstly using hand drawn charts and then on those new-fangled things called computers). For 18 months after reading this book I spent 2 hours a day, 7 days a week, scanning hundreds of commodity charts for the setups discussed. Ask Trish – she almost left me.

I built countless spreadsheets and took notes and made observations. Some patterns I discarded, but others I adjusted. I added additional techniques such as the Traders Trick Entry (which I learned from a Joe Ross book[6]). Slowly but surely a complete trading plan emerged and in my first full year of trading I made a 40% return.

We still use those techniques today at The Chartist.

Long Term Secrets to Short Term Trading by **Larry Williams**

This book contains some serious statistical flaws due to data mining but from an ideas perspective it is invigorating. I was eager to put some of his patterns to the test, but quickly found the flaw. By the time I read the book, many of the patterns had fallen flat because of the sample size bias.

However, if you're a thinking trader, if you're willing to innovate and test differently, then there is gold to be had. Take the Oops! pattern – possibly the best known around the world and now completely arbitraged out due to the book's popularity.

But reworking that pattern slightly made a big difference.

For example, rather than buying as prices broke back into the prior days range, why not buy on the open itself? Better still, the risk adjusted reward could be enhanced by using the size of the opening gap as a setup trigger.

Then I realized that the opening gaps across Asia were bigger than the US markets so I was   able to apply the same setup on the Australian open, the Taiwan open, the Japan open and then the Hong Kong open. The gap faded as Europe opened.

---

[6] https://tradingeducators.com/free-ebook-traders-trick-entry

It's been 20 years or so since I found those patterns – and they still work today.

Market Wizards I and *Market Wizards* II by Jack Schwager

I vividly remember sitting beside my mentor when she was handed a copy of *Market Wizards* by our boss. She knew some of the people featured in the book, but it was a few years later before I read it myself.

The importance lies in the theme of the book, almost between the lines, if you like.

How these traders failed yet continued to push forward. How they doubted themselves. How others doubted them.

The *Market Wizard* books taught me the psychological issues affecting traders and, more importantly, me. As a result, I had several sessions with a psychologist to understand my reactions to the markets and maybe more importantly my reactions to myself.

I've tried to pass on this information in my own books.

Have you taken parts of a trading book and made them your own?

Or are they trophies on your trading shelf?

Nick Radge

Who Wants to be a Billionaire?

I wanna be a billionaire so *@#&ing bad
Buy all the things I never had
I wanna be on the cover of Forbes magazine
Smiling next to Oprah and the Queen

So sings Bruno Mars in the song *Billionaire* by Travie McCoy

It wasn't Forbes but it was the BRW Rich List I was flicking through recently. I do it every year just to see if one of my old mates is still there.

We had lunch together 25 years ago when he wasn't worth $300m. I'm quite sure I paid.

Then he went down one road, and I went down another.

Regrets? No.

But not so for many wanna-be traders.

They get caught up in the hype of the easy profit, the lifestyle of a billionaire trader (whatever that is). They get sucked in by the spruikers shouting "Turn $17 into $468,000 in 2-months!"

Or "The secrets to doubling your money every month!"

It's always compelling to focus on someone else's trading success. How they're Commsec's largest client. How they've bought the waterfront mansion on the back of one great trade. How they make more money in a day than you make in a year pushing the cart.

But it can make you feel lousy about your own situation.

And it can also make you try and speed things up. Rush headlong into the markets without a plan. Make dumb trades. Take excessive risks.

But what so many forget is that every great trader, at one point, was just trying to make a profit too. They were once trying to go from losing to breakeven and then breakeven to minor profitability.

They too took small steps once upon a time.

All that matters is what you're doing, not what anyone else is doing. Focus on running and growing your own trading business rather than being a voyeur.

Maybe change the tune in your head from Bruno Mars to Confucius:

It does not matter how slowly you are going as long as you don't stop.

Now, my old buddy owes me lunch. Paris sounds nice.

Nick Radge

The Problem with Fishing

Over the years I have worked hard on calming my mind. Lowering the internal chatter. Stopped constantly checking stock prices, P&L statements, and reading the media   .

I read fiction. I rarely read trading books these days.

And I used to play a lot of golf.

The problem with golf was that my score was highly correlated with my age – it was heading in one direction. I needed math skills on the golf course more than when I was trading.

I played golf to take my mind off trading, but it stopped working.

So, I took up fishing.

My math skills aren't required so my mind stays calm. Problem solved...

Now the thing with fishing is that I rarely catch any fish.

The lures I was using clearly weren't any good, so I went to the local fishing store and bought more.

They didn't work either.

Maybe it was the rod? The reel? Or the line?

Back to the fishing store. A keen novice with a credit card – I'll take one of everything.

Buy some magazines. Watch YouTube videos incessantly. Visit fishing forums. Join the local fishing club.

Still no joy. The fishing gear was taking over the house. The downstairs bathroom became the 'fishing shed'. Trish didn't complain until the hooks were a danger to the grandkids.

So, I built a fishing shed. Well, I didn't (that's another story for Trish to tell). The builder did.

Maybe it's a scam perpetuated by the fishing stores? Perhaps there aren't any fish, but they'll sell me fishing gear anyway.

The Holy Grail of fishing is out there somewhere. I just haven't bought it yet.

Sound familiar?

The Slow Chef

Many years ago, I decided to make a concerted effort to do more cooking. Well, start cooking was more like it.

We're talking about a bloke who lived at home until he got married. I could handle a barbeque, although that was about it (I did go on a muffin making foray once...).

Trish was obviously very supportive, perhaps a tad too much. So keen she started a blog called The Slow Chef with the aim "...to follow the journey of Nick from Noosa as he learns how to cook."

The Slow Chef? What the...

Trish will tell you it's because I was slow taking up the whole cooking thing.

But it could also mean that I'm also a little slow upstairs.

Or that I'm slow at doing the actual cooking gig itself.

Which could be closer to the truth.

Let's face it, there is a lot to think about. Writing an ingredients list, navigating the supermarket aisles in search of said ingredients, trying to find things in the kitchen, prep work, the actual cooking, refining the taste and then serving.

This little brain operates in batches. Like most men it functions nicely when handling one thing at a time. I'm not about to try step-4 ahead if step-3 to speed up the process.

One misstep and we go from Duck Ragu to some weird tasting stomach-turning chowder concoction that tastes like spam mixed with jellied spaghetti.

Which is why I respectfully follow the proven recipe.

Here are some ingredients for a proven trading recipe:

1x Moving Average; 200

1x Bollinger Band; 1.0

1x ATR set to 10.
Lookback set to 10.
15 positions.
10% risk per position.
Sprinkle of time.

Combine ingredients and stir.

By using these ingredients and following a proven recipe I discovered the best trading strategy I have developed in my 35-years of trading.

A good recipe is the same as a proven trading plan. It needs to be followed every step of the way.

The Slow Chef – Part 2

I did try my hand at cooking before Trish and I were married. The outcome scarred me for many years and quite frankly it's a miracle she even considered me worthy of marriage from that point on.

Newly moved in together and unsupervised I decided to cook up some tasty muffins from a recipe I found.

How bad could it get?

I dutifully made the mixture as per the instructions and started carefully placing the batter into the muffin tray. The dilemma I immediately faced was that I had enough mixture for 24 muffins, but a tray that only handled 6.

Naturally I filled the 6...and threw the rest in the bin. It wouldn't fit, so why keep it?

I know, I know. Idiot.

When Trish came home I proudly presented my 6 muffins. Of course, the tone of the conversation changed somewhat when I pointed out the problem with the baking tray. She checked the bin and flipped the proverbial lid.

I get it now! But heck, I just didn't see it then.

Those defining moments of clarity occur everywhere, including investing and trading in the stock market. Defining moments where you gain real insight and wisdom.

Trailing stop losses to avoid another GFC disaster. Understanding positive expectancy. Adjusting your positions to maximise returns. Finding a repeating pattern that offers an exceptional edge.

Sometimes these Aha! moments are enough to change your life.

They can be big or small, surprising and inspiring. Sometimes they can be funny, or, as in my case, a bit sad.

There's A Monster in The Bed

I remember when I was very young, I'd hear noises in the night.

I'd do 'the walk' – you know the one that most 4-year old's do. Sprinting down the hall to your parents' room and safety from the monsters lurking outside.

I'd stand at the side of Mum's bed until she woke. I didn't dare stand on my father's side.

Of course, a small prod here and there helped wake her. Or a random cough.

She was obviously a very deep sleeper because sometimes she never awoke (Oh, please! – she knew damn well I was there).

Now we have a sweet 4 year old stay with us once a month and she does the same walk. Her wakeup call is a bit of deep breathing – usually within a few centimeters of Trish's left ear.

After a groggy discussion we conclude there are no monsters lurking and we can all go back to bed.

I love these lines from *Reminiscences of a Stock Operator* by Edwin Lefèvre[7]:

> "I can't sleep" answered the nervous one.
> "Why not?" asked the friend.
> "I am carrying so much cotton that I can't sleep thinking about. It is wearing me out. What can I do?"
> "Sell down to the sleeping point", answered the friend.

The trading monsters also lurk during the night. They've certainly visited me before.

If they visit you, exit positions or reduce exposure until you find your sleeping point.

---

[7] Lefèvre E., 2005, *Reminiscences of a Stock Operator,* John Wiley & Sons (US)

Dial Before You Dig

A shovel is used to dig holes. Unfortunately, a lot of people dig holes in inappropriate places...like the stock market.

Taking quick profits and not allowing the trend to run. Dig.

Hanging onto losing trades in the hope they will turn around. Dig.

Punting on stocks that are being talked up by the media or taxi drivers. Dig.

Taking excessive risk on individual trades. Dig.

It's only when they are buried with little to no trading capital left that they call me.

Sometimes it's too late.

If you've dug yourself into a hole, you need to:

1. acknowledge you're in a hole
2. stop digging
3. call me

Or better still, dial BEFORE you dig.

Stop digging and start building.

Why Useful beats Amazing

Winning Lotto would be amazing.

Shooting a hole in one would be amazing.

Having a bank account like Warren Buffett would be amazing.

But all are grossly unrealistic.

Having a job is useful. Just staying on the fairway is useful (note to self).

Making each trade, one at a time, day after day, month after month, year after year, is useful.

You get amazing results just doing useful things over the longer term.

Some Sage Advice from Sgt Schultz

Who would have thought that a piece of advice from a Stalag 13 guard some 50 years ago would be so useful to investors today?

Let me tell you about a guy I knew in 2002. Let's call him Harold.

He was trying to manage his own super fund which was worth around $400,000 at the time.

It was probably worth much the same over 10 years on, which makes sense because he was simply too scared to place a trade or invest – in anything.

Harold reads and absorbs all things Doom & Gloom.

You know the newsletters and blogs I'm talking about – global depression, Gold to $5,000, Dow to 500, hoard Bitcoin where you can hide from the Government. The Fed have us all sewn up. The Freemasons control Oil and pushing prices to the moon (which they also own).

Sure, fear sells.

But Harold missed one of the greatest bull markets of our generation. And you cannot afford to miss those.

How expensive was the Doom & Gloom advice for Harold?

His $400,000 after 10 years would have been worth $960,000, so about $560,000 worth of growth. That's a serious contribution to any SMSF.

Sure, have an opinion. Read a newsletter or two. Scan the socials. Watch and wonder what's happening up there on the moon.

But remember it's all just noise and it can be expensive.

So next time you're making investment decisions amongst the noise, remember Sgt Schultz's advice…

"I see nothing!"

Managing Disappointment as a Share Trader

Disappointment manifests itself in many ways when trading or investing. It's one of those psychological traits that must be overcome in order to move forward to achieve our longer-term goals.

Generally, disappointment stems from having an expectation about what the future holds. In its simplest form it's an expectation about a trade or scenario that doesn't come to fruition. This can result in large losses when we hold off realising a small loss whilst attempting to prove our expectations right.

Not realising a loss is an attempt to delay disappointment.

Another type of disappointment is when a stock tags your stop loss and subsequently reverses and continues its merry way without you. We can create a theory that someone was out to target our stop, that the market is rigged. These excuses are complete garbage, but it enables us to pass the blame and avoid disappointment.

Here is a trade from the Growth Portfolio. Not only did we get stopped at almost the absolute low of the dip, but the stock made its way to new highs.

CHC.au - Daily 25/02/2022
Open 16.95,
Hi 17.105,
Lo 16.1,
Close 16.57 (3.7%)
Close = 16.5700, Trailing Stop level = {EMPTY}

Of course, we can only realise this in hindsight. Had we known at the time that within a few weeks the stock would be higher we'd have held on, but we can never know what the future holds. We can only act on current information.

To deal with disappointment it's imperative to understand that a single trade will not make or break you as a trader. Every trade is a single step toward allowing the law of large numbers and positive expectancy to do its job. There will always be another opportunity to exploit our edge so long as we continue to follow the strategy over the longer term.

Points to remember:

1. You cannot predict the future, nor change the past, but you can manage the present.
2. Next 1000 trades. A single trade will not make you or break you.
3. Have no expectations and endure no disappointment.

Power Setups® Playbook

An Introduction to Discretionary Trading

Discretionary Trading is the use of various chart patterns to identify low risk opportunities. These cannot be programmed into a computer, but by using correct trading principles we are able to create an edge over the longer term. Being a discretionary trader allows you to be completely in charge of the trading process.

HISTORY

You may have read the book or even heard the intriguing story about a young ballroom dancer named Nicolas Darvas who traded $25,000 into $2 million dollars in 18 months by using the stock market. In today's terms that would be worth well over $20 million!

Even though this book, *How I Made 2,000,000 in the Stock Market*, was written back in the 60's the simple principles and techniques remain valid today - and we continue to use them successfully.

The following chart shows the setup Nicolas Darvas used to trade back in the 1940's, but here through the latter stages of 2021 it enabled us to make a tidy profit.

Darvas identified a naturally occurring pattern caused by normal human emotion. He then followed along, riding the trends, repeating the process, and making millions of dollars doing so.

The Chartist's short-term strategies, known as the Power Setups®, use this method in the Australian and US stock market.

If there is any secret to this method it would be: cut your losses and let your profits run. This principle has been profitable for decades and continues to be so today.

MY OWN "AH-HA" MOMENT THAT TOOK 18,000 HOURS

Back in the early 90s and well before I'd heard of Nicolas Darvas, I had been tinkering with basic trading techniques, namely moving average crossovers. But one day I came across a book called Pattern Probability Strategy (PPS Trading System) by Curtis Arnold and I had my very own 'light bulb' moment.

Curtis Arnold's methods resonated with me and made complete sense.

Like Darvas, Arnold explored a variety of low-risk chart patterns but then he mathematically tested them over an extended period whilst compiling extensive data on the performance of each. For 18 months I spent over 2 hours a day, 7 days a week, taking each of his patterns and tested them manually across global futures markets. Doing this by hand allowed me to define certain traits and characteristics of each, as well as refining entries and exits to suit my personality.

These patterns are now the basis of how we trade the ASX and US Power Setups® Discretionary Portfolios and can be found below.

Playbook Patterns

ASCENDING TRIANGLE

This is a bullish continuation pattern best traded in strongly upward trending markets. The pattern is best recognised by the flat top of the triangle and four internal swing points. Ideally volume should be declining during its construction.

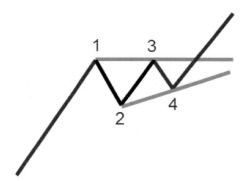

DESCENDING TRIANGLE

Opposite to the Ascending Triangle, this Descending Triangle is a bearish continuation pattern best traded during strong down trends. It is recognised by its flat bottom and four internal swing points. Volume should decline during its construction.

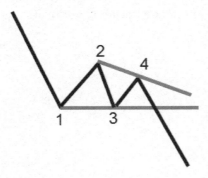

SYMMETRICAL TRIANGLE

This is a continuation pattern and can be found in both bullish and bearish markets. Whilst not as strong as the Ascending or Descending patterns it can still be very useful during strong trends. Recognised by its coiling action and ideally declining volume.

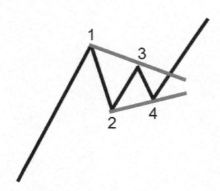

RECTANGLE (DARVAS BOX)

Found in both bullish and bearish markets and recognised by its parallel upper and lower boundaries. This is a continuation pattern and ideally should be traded in the direction of the prevailing trend although can be traded against. Volume should contract during construction.

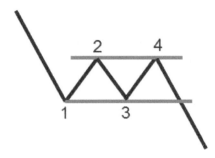

HIGH TIGHT FLAG

Quite possibly the most powerful continuation pattern and certainly should be included in ones trading arsenal. This is a very tiny pause in a very strong trend. Ideally price action leading into the pattern should be impulsive with limited dips. Can last under 5 days.

RESISTANCE LINE

Usually located in an uptrend, although not necessarily in a strong market environment. Recognised by a distinctive horizontal barrier that is touched on a minimum of 3 occasions. The more the barrier is touched the strong the prevailing breakout will usually be.

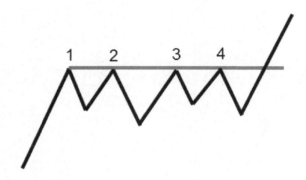

RESISTANCE LINE RETEST

On many occasions after a strong line of resistance is broken price will return to the breakout level. This is known as a retest and can offer a new entry point and on many occasions, one with very low risk. A common setup for professional traders.

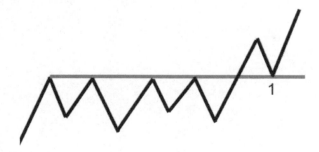

SUPPORT LINE

Usually located in a downtrend, although not necessarily in a strong market environment. Recognised by a minimum of 3 touches of a horizontal barrier below prevailing prices. Can also be seen after sustained uptrend as part of a trend reversal formation.

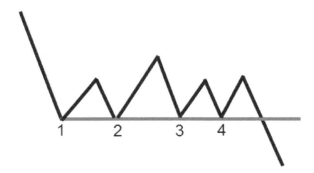

SUPPORT LINE RETEST

A powerful pattern in bearish market environments is a retest of an old support line after an initial breakdown. Many investors look to buy the dip and can briefly force a minor reaction against the trend. A perfect trap.

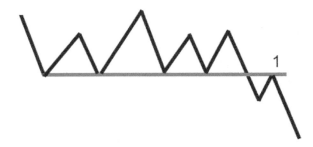

BASE BREAKOUT

After a long down trend or sudden capitulation, a stock may move sideways for an extended period of time as sellers finally get bored and exit. However, the stock is being accumulated and will rise once sellers exit.

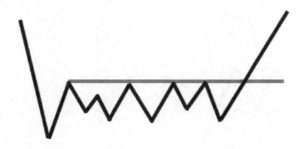

A-B-C or ZIG-ZAG

A common pattern in both up and down trends. A distinctive 3-wave pause in trend where the distances of both -a and -c are of similar length and symmetry. Low volume is ideal during the pattern and best traded using a profit target set at 2% above/below the start of the pattern.

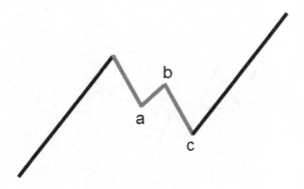

HEAD & SHOULDERS BOTTOM

A worthy pattern to pursue and one that is preceded by a sustained down trend. Recognised by 3 distinct troughs of which the middle is lower than the outside two. Ideally volume into the LS should be high and then declining into the other troughs, especially the RS.

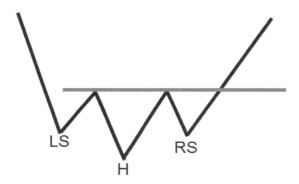

HEAD & SHOULDERS TOP

A common topping pattern following on from a sustained uptrend. Recognised by 3 distinct peaks of which the middle peak is higher than the outside two. Can be a sign of distribution and start of a new trend lower. Can offer various entry points.

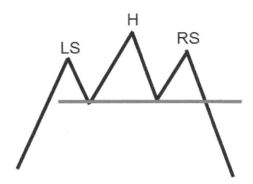

TYPE-A BULLISH DIVERGENCE

There are 3 types of divergences but the Type-A is, in our view, the strongest. It is also the only pattern that uses a corresponding indicator. Price action makes two lows of which the second low is below the first. The indicator makes two lows but the second is higher than the first.

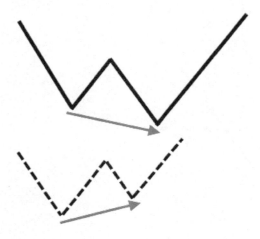

TYPE-A BEARISH DIVERGENCE

This is a bearish reversal pattern whereby price makes two peaks, the second of which is higher than the first. The indicator makes two peaks, of which the second is lower than the first. The opposing peaks create the divergence that operates like a rubber band.

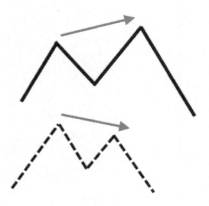

FALLING WEDGE

A bullish pattern found in a strong uptrend. It is seen as a weak attempt at a selloff but is usually on low volume and presents choppy price action. Differs from a flag as it tends toward an extra internal price swing and it coils inward.

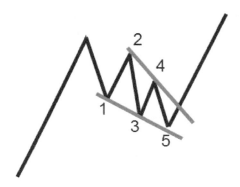

RISING WEDGE

A bearish pattern found in a downtrend. This is a weak attempt at the stock to bounce and is best identified by 5 internal swings in a choppy, coiling action. Pattern becomes more powerful when volume is low.

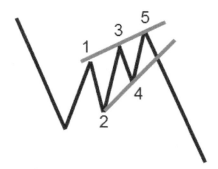

Glossary

ABC

Elliot wave terminology for a three-wave countertrend price movement. Wave A is the first price wave against the trend of the market. Wave B is a corrective wave to Wave A. Wave C is the final price move to complete the countertrend price move. Elliott wave followers study A and C waves for price ratios based on numbers from the Fibonacci series.

Accumulation

Accumulation is the addition to a trader's original market position. The first of three distinct phases in a major trend in which investors are buying.

Adaptive Filter

Adaptive filter is smoothing and/or forecasting prices with continuously updated weighting of past prices.

Advance Decline Line

Each day's number of declining issues is subtracted from the number of advancing issues. The net difference is positive or subtracted from the running sum if the difference is negative.

Adverse Excursion

Adverse Excursion is loss attributable to price movement against the position in any one trade.

Andrews Method

Andrews Method is a technique whereby a technician will pick an extreme low or high to use as a pivot point and draw a line, called the median line, from the point that bisects a line drawn through the next corrective phase that occurs after the pivot point.

Arbitrage

Arbitrage is the simultaneous purchase and sale of two different, however closely related securities to take advantage of a disparity in their prices.

At-the-money

Option whose strike price is nearest the current price of the underlying deliverable.

Average Directional Movement Index (ADX)

Average Directional Movement Index was developed by J. Welles Wilder measuring market trend intensity.

Average True Range

Average True Range is a moving average of the true range.

Back Testing

Back Testing is a strategy tested on historical data and then applied to new data to check for consistency.

Basis

Basis is the difference between spot (cash) prices and the futures contract price.

Basis Points

Basis Points are a measure of yields on bonds and notes (ie. one basis point equals 0.01% of yield).

Basket Trades

Basket trade refers to large transactions made up of a number of different stocks.

Beta

Beta is the measure of volatility that tells how much a stock moves in relation to an index or average.

Black Box

Black Box is a proprietary, computerised trading system whose rules are not disclosed or readily accessible.

Black- Scholes Option Pricing Model

Black- Scholes Option Pricing Model was developed to estimate the market value of option contracts.

Block Trades

Block trades are large transactions of a particular stock sold as a unit.

Blow- Off Top

Blow- Off Top refers to a steep and rapid increase in price followed by a steep and rapid drop in price.

Bracketing

Bracketing refers to the trading range market or a price region that is non-trending.

Breakaway Gap

When a tradable exits a range by trading at price levels that leaves a price area where no trading occurs on a bar chart. These gaps appear at the completion of important chart formations.

Breakout

Breakout refers to the point when the market price moves out of the trend channel.

CAGR (Compounded Average Growth Rate)

CAGR is the annual return of a strategy or investment compounded.

Call Option

Call option is a contract that gives the buyer of the option the right but not the obligation to take delivery of the underlying security at a specific price within a certain time.

Candlestick Charts

Candlestick charts are a charting method, originally from Japan, in which the high and low are plotted as a single line and are referred to as shadows. The price range between the open and the close is plotted as a narrow rectangle and is referred to as the body. If the close is above the open, the body is white. If the close is below the open, the body is black.

Catastrophe Stop

A Catastrophe Stop is an absolute level where positions must be exited because existing exits have not yet activated.

Chakin Oscillator

Chakin Oscillator is an oscillator created by subtracting a 10 day from a three-day EMA of accumulation/distribution line.

Channel

In charting, a price channel contains prices throughout a trend. There are three basic ways to draw channels: parallel, rounded and channels that connect lows or highs.

Chaos Theory

Chaos theory describes the behaviour of non-linear systems. A subset of non-linear dynamics analysis, chaos theory is a branch of mathematics focusing on irregular and complex behaviour that has an underlying order.

Christmas Tree Spread

Christmas Tree Spread is a simultaneous purchase and writing of option with either a different strike price or expiration date or combination of the two.

Closed Trades

Closed trades are positions that have been either liquidated, sold or offset.

Compound Average Growth Rate (CAGR)

CAGR is the annual return of the strategy or investment compounded.

Confidence Factor

Confidence Factor measures the degree of likelihood that a rule is correct, which may reflect the percentage of times that it has proven to be correct in the past or just a subjective measure of our confidence in its degree of reliability.

Confirmation

Confirmation is the indication that at least two indices, in the case of Dow theory the industrials and the transportation, corroborate a trend or a turning point.

Congestion Area or Pattern

Congestion area or pattern is a series of trading days in which there is no visible progress in price.

Consolidation

Consolidation is also known as a congestion period. A pause that allows market participants to re-evaluate the market and sets the stage for the next price move.

Continuation Chart

A chart in which the price scale for the data for the end of a given contract and the data for the beginning of the next contract are merged in order to ease the transition of one contract to the next.

Convergence

Convergence is when futures prices and spot prices come together at the expiration.

Coppock Curve

Coppock curve is a long-term price momentum indicator: a 10-month weighted moving average of the sum of the 14-month rate of change and the 11-month rate of change for the DJIA.

Correction

Correction is any price reaction within the market leading to an adjustment by as much as one-third to two-thirds of the previous gain.

Corrective Wave

Corrective wave is a wave or cycle of waves moving against the current impulse trend's direction.

Countermove

Countermove refers to the price bar showing movement opposite to the direction of the prior period (ie. a retracement).

Cover

Cover is repurchasing a contract sold before.

Covered Write

Writing a call against a long position in the underlying stock. By receiving a premium, the writer intends to realise additional return on the underlying common stock or gain some element of protection from a decline in the value of that underlying stock.

Credit Spread

Credit Spread is the difference in value of two options, where the value of one sold exceeds the value of one purchased.

Cup with Handle

Cup with Handle refers to the accumulation pattern observed on bar charts and lasts from seven to 65 weeks; the cup is in the shape of a U and the handle is usually more than one or two weeks in duration. The handle is a downward drift with low trading volume from the right side.

Curve-Fitting

Curve-Fitting is developing complicated rules that map known conditions.

Cycle

Variation where a point of observation returns to its origin.

Daily Range

Daily Range is the difference between high and low price in one trading day.

Dead-Cat Bounce

Dead-Cat Bounce is a market rebound that sees prices recover and come back up.

Debit Spread

Debit Spread is the difference in value of two options, where the value of the long position exceeds the value of the short.

Deep-in-the-Money

Deep-in-the-Money is a call option with the strike well below the current price of the underlying instrument or a put option with the strike well above the current price of the underlying instrument.

Delta

Delta is the amount by which the price of an option changes for every dollar move in the underlying instrument.

Delta-Hedged

Delta-Hedged an options strategy that protects an option against small price changes in the option's underlying instrument.

Delta-Neutral

Options/options or options/underlying instrument position constructed so it is relatively insensitive to the price movement of underlying instruments.

Delta Position

Delta Position is the measure of option price vs. underlying futures contract or stock price.

Derivatives

Derivatives are financial contracts the value of which depend on the value of the underlying instrument – commodity, bond, equity, currency or a combination.

Directional Movement Index (DMI)

Developed by J. Welles Wilder, DMI measures market trend.

Divergence

Divergence is when two or more averages or indices fail to show confirming trends.

Double Bottom (Top)

Double Bottom (top) shows price action of a security or market average where it has declined (advanced) two times to the same approximate level, indicating the existence of a support (resistance) level and a possibility that the downward (upward) trend has ended.

Efficient Market Theory

Efficient Market Theory in which all known information is already discounted by the market and reflected in the price.

Elliott Wave Theory

Elliott Wave Theory refers to pattern recognition technique published by Ralph Nelson Elliott in 1939, holding that the stock market follows a rhythm or pattern of five waves up and three waves down to form a complete cycle of eight waves. Three waves down are referred to as a correction of the preceding five up.

Envelope

Bands that surround a symbol or indicator.

Exercise

Exercise is the process by which the holder of an option makes or receives delivery of shares of the underlying security.

Exit

Exit is the point at which a trader closes out of a trade.

Expert Systems

Expert Systems are rule-driven systems that cannot learn as the result of new information being fed into its system as opposed to neural networks, which can.

Expiration

Expiration is the last day on which an option can be traded.

Exponential Moving Average

Exponential Moving Average is similar to a simple moving average but gives greater weight to the latest data and responds to changes faster than a simple moving average.

Exponential Smoothing

Exponential Smoothing is a Mathematical statistical method of forecasting that assumes future price action is a weighted average of past periods; a mathematic series in which greater weight is given to more recent price action.

Fade

Selling a rising price or buying a falling price. A trader fading an up opening would be short, for example.

Failure Swings

Failure swings is the inability of price to reaffirm a new high in an uptrend or a new low in a downtrend.

Failure

In Elliott theory, a five-wave pattern of movement in which the fifth impulse wave fails to move above the end of the third, or in which the fifth wave does not contain the five sub waves.

Fibonacci Ratio

Fibonacci Ratio is the ratio between any two successive numbers in the Fibonacci sequence, known as phi(f). The ratio of any number to the next higher number is approximately 0.618 (known as the Golden Meanor Golden Ratio), and to the lower number approximately 1.618 (the inverse of the

Golden Mean), after the first four numbers of the series. Three important ratios that the series provides are 0.618, 1.0 and 1.618.

Fibonacci Sequence

Sequence of numbers (0,1,2,3,5,8,13,21,34,55,89,144,233...) discovered by Italian mathematician Leonardo de Pisa in the 13th century and the mathematical basis of the Elliott wave theory. This occurs where the first two terms of the sequence are 0 and 1 and each successive number in the sequence is the sum of the previous two numbers. Technically a sequence and not a series.

Fill

Fill is an executed order; sometimes the term refers to the price at which an order is executed.

Filter

Filter is a device or program that separates data, signal or information in accordance with specified criteria.

Flag

Sideways market price action with a slight price drift counter to the direction of the main trend (ie. a consolidation phase).

Front Month

Front Month is the first expiration month in a series of months.

Fundamental Analysis

Fundamental Analysis is an analytical method by which only the sales, earnings and the value of a given tradable asset may be considered.

Fundamentals

Theory that holds that stock market activity may be predicted by looking at the relative data and statistics of a stock as well as the management of the company and its earnings.

Future Volatility

Future Volatility is a prediction of what volatility may be like in the future.

Gamma

Gamma is the degree by which the delta changes with respect to changes in the underlying instrument's price.

Gann's Square of 9

Gann's Square of 9 is a trading tool that relates numbers, such as a stock price, to degrees on a circle.

Gann Theory

Various analytical techniques developed by legendary trader W.D. Gann.

Gap

Gap refers to the day in which the daily range is completely above or below the previous day's daily range.

Golden Mean or Golden Ratio

Ratio of any two consecutive numbers in the Fibonacci sequence, equal to 0.618; an important proportion that is a phenomenon in music, art, architecture and biology.

Golden Section

Golden Section refers to any length divided so that the ratio of the smaller to the larger part is equivalent to the ratio between the larger part and the whole and is always 0.618.

Greeks

Jargon; a loose term encapsulating a set of risk variables used by options traders.

Head and Shoulders

Head and Shoulders refers to when the middle price peak of a given tradeable is higher than those around it.

Herrick Payoff Index

Index requiring two inputs, one of which is a smoothing factor known as the multiplying factor; the other is the value of a one-cent move.

Historic Volatility

Historic Volatility refers to how much contract price has fluctuated over a past period; usually calculated by taking a standard deviation of price changes over a period.

Hook Day

Hook Day is a trading day in which the open is above/below the previous day's high/low and the close is below/above the previous day's close with a narrow   range.

Implied Volatility

Volatility computed using actual market prices of an option contract and one of several pricing models.

Impulse

Impulse is a sharply defined change in a series of input data being studied, such as market prices or volume.

Impulse Wave

Wave or cycles of waves that carry the current trend further in the same direction.

In-the-Money

In-the-Money is a call option whose strike is lower than the stock or future's price, or a put option whose strike is higher than the underlying tradeable's price.

Intrinsic Value

Intrinsic Value is the portion of an option's premium that is represented when the cash market price is greater than the exercise price; a known constant equal to the difference between the strike price and underlying market price.

January Effect

January Effect refers to the tendency for securities prices to recover in January after tax related selling is completed before the previous year's end.

Lag

Number of data points that a filter, such as a moving average, follows or trails the input price data. Also, in trading and time series analysis, lag refers to the time difference between one value and another. Though lag specifically refers to one value being behind or later than another, generic use of the term includes values that may be before or after the reference value.

LEAPS

LEAPS is an acronym for long term equity anticipation securities, which are long term listed options, with maturities that can be as long as two and a half years.

Least Squares Method

Least Squares Method is a Technique of fitting a curve close to given points that minimizes the sum of the squares of the deviations of the given points from the curve.

Leg

One side of a spread.

Limit Move

Limit Move is a change in price that exceeds the limits set by the exchange on which the contract is traded.

Limit Order

Order to buy or sell when a price is fixed.

Limit Up; Limit Down

Commodity exchange restrictions on the maximum up or down movements permitted in the price for a commodity during any trading session day.

Locked Limit

Locked Limit is a market that, if not restricted, would seek price equilibrium outside the limit but, instead, moves to the limit and ceases to trade.

Long

Establishing ownership of the responsibilities of a buyer of a tradeable (ie. holding securities in anticipation of a price increase in that security).

Lookback Interval

Lookback Interval is the number of periods of historical data used for observation.

MACD

See Moving Average Convergence/Divergence.

Managed Futures

Managed Futures refers to a fund that uses the futures market as its primary asset.

Margin

In stock trading, an account in which purchase of stock may be financed with borrowed money; in futures trading, the deposit placed with the clearinghouse to assure fulfilment of the contract. This amount varies daily and is settled in cash.

Marked to Market

At the end of each business day, open positions carried in an account held at a brokerage are credited or debited funds based on the settlement of the open positions that day.

Market If Touched

Resting order with floor broker that becomes a market order to be executed if the trigger is hit.

Market Maker

Market Maker refers to a broker or bank prepared to make a two-way price to purchase or sell for a security or currency.

Market on Close

Order specification that requires the broker to get the best price available on the close of trading, usually during the last five minutes of trading.

Market Order

Instructions to the broker to immediately sell to the best available bid or to buy from the best available offer.

Market Risk

Market Risk refers to the uncertainty of returns attributable to fluctuation of the entire market.

Market Sentiment

Crowd psychology, typically a measurement of bullish or bearish attitudes among investors and traders.

Market Timing

Market timing refers to using analytical tools to devise entry and exit methods.

Market Value

Company value determined by investors, obtained by multiplying the current price of company stock by the common shares outstanding.

Martingale

From roulette, a tactical system that requires doubling your bet after each loss, so that winning once you recoup the amount originally bet.

Maximum Adverse Excursion

Historical measurement of the closed losing trades versus the closed profitable trades of a trading system. Used to determine the stop-loss that can be used that will allow winning trades to remain (ie. the extreme unfavourable price level reached for both profitable and unprofitable trades).

Mathematical Edge

Mathematical Edge is a calculation to show how your strategy will make money before you ever place a trade.

Mean

Mean or average. When the sum of the values is divided by the number of numbers.

Mean Deviation

Average absolute value of the difference between the population of numbers and the mean.

Mental Stop-Loss

Stop-loss order kept in your head instead of instructing your broker.

Momentum

Momentum is a time series representing change of today's price from some fixed number of days back in history.

Momentum Filter

Momentum Filter refers to measure of change, derivative or slope of the underlying trend in a time series. Implemented by first applying a low-pass filter to the data and then applying a differencing operation to the results.

Momentum Indicator

Market indicator utilizing price and volume statistics for predicting the strength or weakness of a current market and any overbought or oversold conditions, and to note turning points within the market.

Moving Average

Moving Average is a mathematical procedure to smooth or eliminate data fluctuations and to assist in determining when to buy and sell. Moving averages emphasise the direction of a trend, confirm trend reversals and smooth price and volume fluctuations that can confuse interpretation of the market; sum of a value plus a selected number of previous values divided by the total number of values.

Moving Average Crossovers

Point where the various moving average lines intersect each other or the price line on a moving average price bar chart. Technicians use crossovers to signal price-based buy and sell opportunities.

Moving Average Convergence/Divergence (MACD)

Crossing of two exponentially smoothed moving averages plotted above and below a zero line. Crossover, movement through the zero, and divergences generate buys and sells.

Naked Put

Writer of a put option not short the underlying security.

Narrow Range Day

Narrow Range Day is a trading day with a smaller price range relative to the previous day's price range.

Near-the-Money

Option with a strike close to the current price of the underlying.

Neckline

Trendline drawn along the support or resistance points of various reversal and consolidation pattern (ie. head and shoulder, double and triple top/bottom formations).

Negative Convergence

Negative Convergence is when two or more averages, indices or indicators fail to show confirming trends.

Net Asset Value

Total market value of all securities contained in a mutual fund; also known as price per share.

Neural Network

Neural Network is an artificial intelligence program capable of learning through a training process of trial and error.

Noise

Noise refers to price and volume fluctuations that can confuse interpretation of market direction.

Non-Trend Day

Non-Trend Day is a narrow range day lacking any discernible movement in either direction.

Normal Distribution

For the purposes of statistical testing, the simulated net returns are assumed to be drawn from a particular distribution. If net returns are drawn from a normal distribution, low and high returns are equally likely, and the most likely net return in a quarter is the average net return.

On-Balance Volume

Plotted as a line representing the cumulative total of volume. The volume from a day's trading with a higher close when compared with the previous day is assigned a positive value, while volume on a lower close from the previous day is assigned a negative value. Traders look for a confirmation of a trend in OBV with the market or a divergence between the two as an indication of a potential reversal.

Open Trades

Open Trades are current trades that are still held active in the customer's account.

Opening Range

Opening Range refers to the range of prices that occur during the first 30 seconds to five minutes of trading, depending on the preference of the individual analyst.

Optimisation

Optimisation refers to the methodology by which a system is developed with rules tailored to fit the data in question precisely.

Oscillator

Oscillator is a technical indicator used to identify overbought and oversold price regions. An indicator that de-trends data, such as price.

Out-of-Sample

Item within the range of a sample that does not conform to the mean of the sample.

Out-of-the-Money

Out-of-the-Money is a call option whose exercise price is above the current market price of the underlying security or futures contract. For example, if a commodity price is $500, then a call option purchased for a strike price of $550 is considered out-of-the-money

Overbought

Overbought refers to market prices that have risen too steeply and too fast.

Overfitting

Parameters of a trading system are selected to return the highest profit over the historical data.

Oversold

Oversold refers to market prices that have declined too steeply and too fast.

Overbought/Oversold Indicator

Indicator that defines when prices have moved too far and too fast in either direction and thus are vulnerable to a reaction.

Parabolic

A non-sustainable price movement, having the form of or relating to a parabola.

Parameter

Variable, set of data, or rule that establishes a format for a model.

Pennants

Short compact wedge accompanied by receding volume.

Pivot Point

In market activity, a price reversal point.

Point and Figure Chart

Price-only chart that plots up prices as X's and down prices as O's. Minimum price recorded is called the box size. Typically, a three-box reversal indicates a change in the direction of prices.

Premium

Premium is the price a buyer pays to an option writer for granting an option contract.

Profit Taking

Profit taking refers to selling tradeables that have appreciated since initial purchase to take advantage of the appreciation.

Program Trading

Trades based on signals from computer programs, usually entered directly from the trader's computer to the market's computer system.

Put Option

Put Option is a contract to sell a specified amount of a stock or commodity at an agreed time at the stated exercise price.

Pyramid

Pyramid refers to increasing   holdings that an investor has by using the most buying power available in a margin account with paper and real profits.

Rally Tops

Rally Tops refers to price level that concludes a short-term rally in an on-going trend.

Random Walk

Random Walk is a theory that says there is no sequential correlation between prices from one day to the next.

Range

Range is the difference between the high and low price during a given period.

Range Extension

In the CBOT Market Profile, a price movement beyond the range set by the initial auction.

Rate of Change

In which today's closing price is divided by the closing price n days ago. Multiply by 100. Subtract 100 from this value.

Ratio

Relation that one quantity bears to another of the same kind, with respect to magnitude or numerical value.

Reaction

Reaction is a short-term decline in price against a prevailing uptrend.

Rectangle

Rectangle refers to a trading area bounded by horizontal, or near horizontal, lines. It can either be a reversal or continuation pattern, depending on the breakout.

Relative Strength

Relative Strength is a comparison of the price performance of a stock to a market index such as S&P 500 stock index.

Relative Strength Index

Relative Strength Index is an indicator invented by J. Welles Wilder and used to ascertain overbought/oversold situations.

Resistance

Price level at which rising prices have stopped rising and either moved sideways or reversed direction.

Resting Order

Resting Order is an order placed with a condition or qualifier but not yet executed.

Retracement

Retracement is price movement in the opposite direction of the previous trend.

Reward-Risk Ratio

Monthly excess return to risk comparison, calculated by dividing alpha by standard deviation. (A ratio better than 0.4 is excellent).

Reversal Gap

Chart formation where the low of the last day is completely above the previous day's range with the close above mid-range and above the open.

Reversal Stop

Reversal is a stop that, when hit, is a signal to reverse the current trading position. Also known as stop and reverse.

Risk (Implied)

In which the formula produces percentage overbought/oversold for contract using price, moving average and option's implied volatility.

Rounding Bottom

Rounding Bottom is a pattern describing the process of a company regrouping after a series of business missteps. The rounding bottom is the end of the downtrend.

Saucer Base

Saucer Base is like a cup and handle formation, but the saucer base is shallower and rounder in shape.

Seasonality

Seasonality is consistent and predictable change in market activity that occurs from consistent and predictable events.

Selling Short

Selling a security and then borrowing the security for delivery with the intent of replacing the security at a lower price. In futures trading, selling short is to assume the responsibility of the seller vs. the buyer.

Serial Correlation

Serial Correlation refers to the systematic relationship between successive observations of a time series.

Simple Moving Average

Arithmetic mean or average of a series of prices over a period.

Slippage

Slippage is the difference between estimated transaction and actual transaction costs.

Smoothing

Simply, a mathematical technique that removes excess data variability while maintaining a correct appraisal of the underlying trend.

Spike

Sharp rise in price in a single day or two; may be as great as 15-30%, indicating the time for an immediate sale.

Spot Month

Spot Month is the current contract month. Also known as the front month.

Spot Prices

Spot Prices are the same as cash price, the price at which a commodity is selling at a particular time and place.

Spread

Trade in which two related tradeables are traded to exploit the relative differences in price change.

Spread Rolls

Spread Rolls refers to using a spread order to bridge the closing of one position and the establishment of a new one.

Spring

Spring refers to a two-day pattern in which on the first day, the market declines below a support point, while the next day sees the market move strongly back up into the congestion area. Also, another term for upthrust; occurs when price moves above a pivot top and a widespread reversal ensues.

Standard Deviation

Square root of the expected value of the square of the difference between a random variable and its mean.

Stochastic Oscillator

Stochastic Oscillator refers to overbought/oversold indicator that compares today's price to a preset window of high and low prices.

Stops

Buy stops are orders placed at a predetermined price over the current price of the market. Sell stops are orders that are placed with a predetermined price below the current price.

Stop and Reverse (SAR)

Stop that, when hit, is a signal to reverse the current trading position. Also known as reversal stop.

Stop-Loss

Stop-Loss is a risk management technique in which the trade is liquidated to halt any further decline in value.

Stop-Running

After a trend, the market will enter a trading range and have a tendency to trade to levels where stop- loss orders have been placed.

Straddle

Straddle refers to a purchase or sale of an equivalent number of puts and calls on an underlying stock with the same exercise price and expiration date.

Strangle

Strangle refers to purchase or sale of an equivalent number of puts and calls on an underlying stock with the same expiration date but a different exercise price.

Strike Price

Strike Price is the price per unit at which the holder of an option may receive or deliver the underlying unit; also known as the exercise price.

Support

Historical price level at which falling prices have stopped falling and either moved sideways or reversed direction; usually seen as a price chart pattern.

Swing Chart

Chart with a straight line drawn from each price extreme to the next price extreme based on set criteria such as percentages or number of days.

Swings

Swings refers to a measurement of movement of the price of a tradeable between extreme highs and lows.

Technical Analysis

Technical Analysis is a form of market analysis that studies demand and supply for securities and commodities based on trading volume and price studies.

Thrust

Thrust is the comparison between the price difference of successively lower pivot bottoms or higher pivot tops.

Tick

Minimum fluctuation of a tradeable, most stocks trade in eighths.

Time Series

Time series is a collection of observations made sequentially in time and indexed by time.

Time Value

Time Value is the difference between the premium paid for an option and the intrinsic value. As the option approaches expiration, the time value erodes, eventually to zero.

Trading Range

Trading range is the difference between high and low prices traded during a period (ie. in commodities, the high/low price limit established by the exchange for a specific commodity for any one day's trading).

Trailing Stop

Stop-loss order that follows the prevailing price trend.

Trend

Trend refers to the tendency of a set of statistical data as related to time.

Trend Channel

Parallel probable price range centred about the most likely price line. Historically, this term has been used to denote the area between the base trendline and the reaction trendline defined by price moves against the prevailing trend.

Trend Day

Trend Day is the day in which the a symbol moves in the same direction for the full day.

Trend Following

Trend Following is positioning oneself   in the direction of the prevailing price movement.

Trendless

Price movement that vacillates to the degree that a clear trend cannot be identified.

Trendline

Line drawn that connects either a series of highs or lows in a trend.

Triangle

A pattern that exhibits a series of narrower price fluctuations over time (ie. top and bottom boundaries need not be of equal length).

Upthrust

Upthrust occurs when price moves above a pivot top and a widespread reversal ensues.

Value Area

Value Area is the price range on the CBOT Market Profile in which approximately 70% of the day's trades occur.

Variable-Length Moving Average

Moving average where the number of periods selected for smoothing is based on a volatility measurement of price.

Vertical Spread

Stock option spread based on simultaneous purchase and sale of options on the same underlying stock with the same expiration months but different strike prices.

Volatility

Volatility is the measure of a stock's tendency to move up and down in price, based on its daily price history over the latest 12 months.

Volume

Shares traded for a given market or tradeable.

Wave

In Elliott wave theory, a sustained move by a market's price in one direction is determined by the reversal points that initiated and terminated it.

Wave Cycle

Impulse wave followed by a correction wave, the impulse wave being made up of five smaller, numbered waves of alternating direction designated 1,2,3,4 and 5, and the correction wave being composed of three smaller alternating waves designated a, b and c.

Wedge

Wedge is a pattern in which two converging lines connect a group of price peaks and troughs.

Whipsaw

Whipsaw refers to losing money on both sides of a price swing.

Williams' %R

Williams' %R is an overbought and oversold indicator that is used to determine market entry and exit points.

Follow Nick Radge on Twitter @thechartist

thechartist.com.au

nickradge.com

Printed in Great Britain
by Amazon

40252379R00097